The Lies of Our Democracy And ... How They Hurt Us

Dave Kocak

Untiliwin Press
Buffalo, New York

Copyright 2019 by Dave Kocak

All right reserved.
Published in the United States

ISBN 978-1-7333831-0-3
E-Book ISBN 978-1-7333831-1-0

First Edition

Dedication

This book is dedicated to my wife Joanne, who inspires me daily, to my great niece Miranda Darone, who keeps me hopeful for the future, and to everyone who seeks the truth and rejects the lies that seem to abound in our modern, electronic lives.

Acknowlegements

To all those friends who have encouraged me, corrected me, and advised me in the writing of this book. This list includes, but is not limited to, Jeff Jones, Mary Jo Kenney, Sara Kemmerer, Dan Murphy, the students in my writing class, and Joe Darone, my favorite brother-in-law.

*"A Problem Well-Stated
Is
A Problem Half Solved."*

Charles Franklin Kettering –
Inventor, Head of General Motors research
1920-1947

Warning

Despite the title, this is not a book about Candidate or President Donald J. Trump. That would be too easy. Donald Trump lied when he announced his candidacy and has lied just about every day since. He proved to be no different as President when he insisted that his inaugural crowd was bigger than President Obama's and that he would have won the popular vote if not for three to five million fraudulent ballots cast. There was absolutely no proof for either of these claims. President Trump will have many books written about him, just not this one.

No, this book is about more significant and enduring lies that have crept into and stayed with the national conversation. It's about things we take for granted that may not be true, and truths that we would rather not mention. It's about myths we perpetuate because they make us feel good. It's about truths that are no longer true.

President Donald Trump will have very little effect on these lies. They are too ingrained into the American psyche, and may endure long after he is gone.

Table of Contents

Warning 07
Table of Contents 09
Foreword 11
Introduction 13

Lie #1: The Solution is Simple 15
Lie #2: Government is not the Solution, Government is the Problem 17
Lie #3: Politicians are the Problem 19

The Five Pillars of American Democracy 21
The First Pillar of Democracy: The First Amendment to the Constitution 21

Section 1: The Military 23
Lie #4: The Military is in Terrible Shape 25
Lie #5: The National Defense Budget is $700 Billion 27
Lie #6: Drone Strikes Eliminate Terrorist Threats While Minimizing Civilian Casualties 29
Lie #7: We Honor and Respect the Military 31

The Second Pillar of Democracy: An Independent Judiciary 35

Section 2: Our Elected Officials 37
Lie #8: We Have Free and Fair Elections 39
Lie #9: One Man, One Vote 43
Lie #10: One Man, One Vote (Kinda) 47

Intermission: Phrases that Lie 49

Section 3: Money, Money, Money 53
Lie #11: Congress Swears an Oath to Defend the Constitution, and the Constitution Alone 55
Lie #12: Attack Waste, Fraud and Abuse to Reduce the Budget Deficit 57
Lie #13: Americans are Overtaxed 61
Lie #14: The Death Tax Hurts Farmers and Small Businessmen 63

Lie #15: A Corporation's Only Duty is to Shareholder Value 67
Lie #16: The Poor are Poor Due to Bad Choices 69
Lie #17: Income Inequality is a Feature of American Capitalism... 73
The Third Pillar of Democracy: Innovation and Entrepreneurship 75
Section 4: Government 77
Lie #18: U.S. Finance leads the World Economy...79
Lie #19: Business is Drowning in Burdensome Regulation... 81
Lie #20: States Rights Counterbalance an Ever-Increasing Federal Government... 83
Lie #21: The Supreme Court is the Final "Law of the Land"... 85
Lie #22: Pro-Choice, Pro-Life Abortion Positions Have Equal Support... 87
Lie #23: We Can Replace Fossil Fuels with Other Forms of Energy... 89
Lie #24: American Exceptionalism?... 91
The Fourth Pillar of Democracy: Immigration 93
Section 5: The Social Fabric of America... 95
Lie #25: We Live in a Post-Racial Society 97
Lie #26: We Want a Country of Equal Opportunity, Not Equal Outcomes 101
Lie #27: Americans do Not Want "Socialized Medicine" like Canada... 103
Lie #28: America is the Moral Leader of the World 107
Lie #29: We are All in this Together 111
Conclusion... 115
The Fifth Pillar of Democracy: Charity 117
Recommended Reading List... 119

Foreword

"My work is not a piece of writing designed to meet the needs of an immediate public, but was done to last forever."
THUCYDIDES ANCIENT GREEK HISTORIAN, HISTORY OF THE PELOPONNESIAN WAR

This is not a work of great scholarship. I am not a great scholar, and you are probably not looking for a scholarly work. You were probably attracted to this book by the thinness of the spine rather than the promise of an intense review of the lies of America. This book is built on the work of scholars, many of whom appear on my recommended reading list at the end. Those books run more than 8,000 pages, plus notes. This book is 100 pages, no notes.

I hope to combine their great scholarship with common sense from a common man to create a book that would make you think about the real problems of our country, and perhaps get excited enough to investigate further. You will be the judge of whether I have succeeded.

"I believe that anyone who claims to know what's going on will lie about the little things too."
NEIL GAIMAN (1960-PRESENT) - AUTHOR, "THE SANDMAN" AND "CORALINE"

Introduction

"In a time of universal deceit, telling the truth is a revolutionary act."
GEORGE ORWELL (1903-1950), AUTHOR "1984"

"We may never know the results of the 2016 election, and what the actual margin of victory may have been." What??!! After 50 secretaries of state certified the election, Kris Kobach, secretary of state for Kansas and chairman of the pompously titled Presidential Advisory Commission on Election Integrity, says that the election count is unknown. Why? How? There is no evidence of election fraud and the margin of the popular vote was 2.8 million votes! This is the lie that started this book.

I'm not a political scientist, a journalist, or a politician. I'm just a sixty-eight year old white guy sports instructor who has paid some attention to politics and government for the last forty years. Truth be told, I'm more liberal than conservative, but mostly moved by falsehoods and stupidity, which both parties seem to have in abundance. Bringing them to your attention may move us closer to actually agreeing on some things in this country and possibly improving the lives of our citizens.

President Trump, (last time he gets mentioned, I promise) with no evidence to support his claim, said that he would have won the popular vote if 3-5 million illegal voters had not voted for Clinton. Kris Kobach claims it's unknowable.

It's hard to imagine a bigger lie told by the winners of an election. I don't believe for a second that Kris Kobach believes it was anything other than a 2.8 million vote win for Clinton. I have absolutely no idea what Donald Trump believes.

This lie is one in a long series of lies, told by Democrats, Republicans, the military, the marketers, and the media. Lastly, we must not forget the citizens of the United States, who have been lying to themselves for a long, long time now. Facts are facts. Opinions are not facts. Beliefs are not facts. Feelings are not facts, and there is no such thing as "alternative facts!" Facts and only facts are facts.

We can't begin to come together as a country until we start telling the truth, and, of course, I mean everyone. That result may only come about when we start calling out the lies and the liars who tell them. Every time we let slide someone's false assertion or ridiculous claim, we destroy the basis for a substantive debate. Every time we allow the media or anyone else to give false equivalence to two less than perfect statements, we diminish the debate.

It turns out Hillary Clinton won the popular vote by 2.9 million votes, not the 2.8 I mentioned earlier. I was wrong. Donald Trump thinks he won the popular vote. He is wrong. We are both wrong, but we are not equally wrong. I was off by 100,000 votes, while Donald Trump was off by 3-5 million votes, with a claim of massive voter fraud. There is no equivalence in the two statements. One is slightly incorrect while the other is dead wrong. And that's where we're going to begin.

> *"It ain't what you don't know that gets you into trouble.*
> *It's what you know for sure that just ain't so."*
> MARK TWAIN (1835-1910), AMERICAN HUMORIST

LIE #1

The Solution is simple...

"For every complex problem there is an answer that is clear, simple and wrong."
H.L. MENCKEN (1880-1956), BALTIMORE, NEWSPAPER COLUMNIST

If you hear a politician or the guy in the proverbial diner or anyone else start their rant about current national problems with "The solution is simple," please walk away. The solution may be many things, but simple is not one of them.

None of our problems has a simple solution. Immigration, poverty, education, inequality - all are complex problems.

If the solutions were simple, they would already have been enacted. To suggest otherwise does a disservice to the honorable men and women who go into government every day to make a positive difference in the lives of Americans.

But just because a problem is complex does not mean that there is nothing that can be done to improve the situation. It may not be the perfect solution, or a complete solution, and it may not be easy to accomplish, but it doesn't mean there is nothing to be done. And, oh yeah, it might come at a political cost. It is simply cowardice to ignore any important problem because there is no political gain. The Affordable Care Act (ACA), also known as Obamacare, comes to mind as an attempt to improve the health insurance situation for millions of Americans, and whether you think it was a good plan or not, it was a bold attempt to accomplish something, and it came at a severe cost, as the 55 House seats lost by the Democrats in the 2010 midterms will attest.

Unfortunately, Republicans were unwilling to participate in the attempt to improve American healthcare. Newt Gingrich, Republican Congressman and eventual Speaker of the House said in 1994, in regards to the Clinton healthcare initiative in that year, that if Democrats managed to put another big social program in place, Republicans would be in the minority for a generation. By campaigning against it, while putting forth no alternative, Republicans defeated the Clinton plan and gained politically, but not one person in the United States received better healthcare for their efforts. Almost twenty years later, their position was the same. Despite attempts to work with Republicans to craft a bipartisan bill, the ACA, with its many failings, passed Congress without one Republican vote. The ACA is better than the current Republican alternative, which is simply to repeal it.

Immigration, income inequality, opioid addiction, and climate change or weather or whatever you want to call it, all come to mind as problems defying simple solutions, but problems to be solved nonetheless. However difficult they may be, they need to addressed.

"I'm opposed to simplistic readings of complicated social phenomena."
MALCOLM GLADWELL (1963-PRESENT), AUTHOR

LIE #2

Government is not the Solution, Government is the problem.

"The essence of Government is power; and power, lodged as it must be in human hands, will ever be liable to abuse."

JAMES MADISON (1751-1836), FOURTH PRESIDENT OF THE U.S.

This statement, so famously uttered by Ronald Reagan in his 1980 presidential campaign, was not true then, and it is not true now. Taken to the extreme, problem-free countries must include Somalia, Libya, and South Sudan. As government-free lawless states, they are some of the most dangerous places in the world. Too extreme an example? Perhaps. There are many other countries with a small government, little taxation, and minimal infrastructure that are equally unappealing. Honduras, Laos, and Congo quickly come to mind.

Regulation, along with taxation, is the price we pay for civilization. Clean water, clean air, safe products, safe streets, and rule of law all come with regulation and taxation. You can't sit on your porch with a gun all day protecting what's yours and inspecting everything that comes into your house, or can you?

Tea Party exclamations of "Keep your government hands off my Medicare!" notwithstanding, we all want and need what a modern government provides. Forget the Libertarian hype of government for defense and police and not much else. A modern society wants and needs a government to do much more.

We want government to help the less-fortunate, help business, help job creation, and administer services well, with as little corruption as possible. By the way, despite the occasional scandal, America is far less corrupt than most other countries.

What we don't want is an overbearing government. Unfortunately, this is a term we have a very hard time defining. My attempt at greater public safety through gun control is your government trying to take away your Second Amendment rights. You see my attempt to stop abortion as an assault on your reproductive freedom. Anti-discrimination laws against LGBTQ persons are an assault on your freedom of religion. And so it goes.

Are taxes the problem? Americans, although they are taxed somewhere near the bottom (31 of 35 nations) of the industrialized world, are overtaxed, or at least they think they are. I guess what it means to be an American is to believe we have the greatest freedoms but we pay too much for them. We really don't want less government, we just want government to cost less.

Perhaps the government is not the problem. Perhaps it is our inability to reach any kind of common ground on many of the issues today.

Going forward with that idea, politicians must be doing a lousy job, whether or not they have the necessary funds to keep the electorate content.

So Lie #3 must be…

LIE #3

Politicians are the problem.

"It is terrible to contemplate how few politicians are hanged."
G.K. CHESTERTON-(1874-1936), BRITISH WRITER

Supposedly, politicians are always the problem. They used to be blamed for not standing up for their principles, always compromising. Now in this age of hyper-partisanship, they get blamed every time they do compromise. Not just blamed, they get "primaried." Primaried is now a verb, and one so new that it doesn't register on my spell check.

I believe it would be better if politicians didn't worry so much about getting re-elected (this may not be a new idea!). We supposedly try to pick men and women of good judgment, but if they use that good judgment in opposition to party or constituents, we call them unresponsive to the will of the people. We question their ability to tell the truth, but when they do, it's all over the evening news, often out of context but surely alienating at least some of their constituents.

Rather than enabling helpful legislation, they too often just worry about re-election. Of course, in order to get re-elected they have to spend money, which makes fundraising first and foremost in their minds and schedules.

Who invented this system that requires politicians to spend half their time begging for money? Politicians, of course. Now I'm hurting my own argument.

Incumbents never want to change the system that put them in office, but until they do, money will rule the day, as they almost always have a fundraising advantage.

The rich have too much influence on politicians, who always need campaign money, and our officials spend way too much time raising money. The public doesn't seem to want to change the system either. Public financing of elections is somehow seen as just another money grab by politicians rather than a power grab by the rich who pay for those elections.

From a purely economic perspective, I believe it is cheaper to pay for campaigns than it is to pay for the contract or tax break that manages to go to a significant contributor because of his political campaign contributions.

In the end, our politicians reflect us, and we get what we deserve.

Having debunked the most common and obvious lies, let's move on to the myths that are keeping America and its citizens from facing our real problems.

> *"A people that elect corrupt politicians, imposters, thieves and traitors are not victims... but accomplices"*
> GEORGE ORWELL (1903-1950) BRITISH AUTHOR "1984"

The Five Pillars of American Democracy

The Founders created a brilliant, but imperfect document in the Constitution, administered by imperfect men, sometimes for their own benefit. Despite that, American democracy is still strong, and throughout this book we will sprinkle in why I believe this to still be true.

In a book based on lies, we need a little sunshine to remove the doom and gloom contained herein.

Pillar #1: The First Amendment to the Constitution

"Congress shall make no law respecting an establishment of religion, or prohibiting the free exercise thereof; or abridging the freedom of speech, or of the press; or the right of the people to peaceably assemble, and to petition Government for a redress of grievances." U.S. Constitution,

Amendment #1

There's a lot here in those 45 words but let's just focus on freedom of the press and freedom of religion. A free press has been a vital part of U.S. democracy since the beginning, although there was a period in the John Adams' administration around 1800 that the Alien and Sedition Acts dampened that free press. The Sedition Act prohibited public opposition to the government and included fines and imprisonment for those who wrote false or malicious writings against the government. More than 20 newspaper editors were arrested. It was not our finest hour. More than any other institution, the press has kept our government in check, for all governments love secrecy. Watergate and The Pentagon Papers are just two examples where American democracy was well served by an investigative press revealing government secrets. This is probably why no administration, no matter how honest, likes the press.

Freedom of religion has a double meaning. Of course it means that government cannot interfere in the free practice of religion, but it also means that religion cannot interfere in government. When either occurs, history has shown that both are corrupted.

Those who would have their religious views become official government policy are ill-prepared for the influence government will have on the practice of their religion. Islamic states are the most obvious modern example of problematic state religions, but Christianity also has a terrible record in this regard going back more than a thousand years.

The United States has managed to remain a religion-neutral country even though many continue to claim it was founded as a Christion nation. It should be noted that nowhere in the Constitution does the word "God" appear and there is no mention of Christianity. Claims that American Muslims wish to impose Islamic law in our country are similar to the claims fifty years ago that John F. Kennedy, if elected to the White House as a Catholic, would take his orders from the Pope.

He did not, and that's why he was assassinated! Just wanted to see if you were paying attention.

"But separation of church and state was never meant to separate God and government."(???)

ALABAMA CHIEF JUSTICE ROY MOORE-(1947-PRESENT)

"I'm completely in favor of the separation of Church and State. My idea is that these two institutions screw us up enough on their own, so both of them together is certain death."

COMEDIAN GEORGE CARLIN (1937-2008)

SECTION I
The Military

"What's the point of having this superb military you are always talking about if you can't use it?"
SECRETARY OF STATE MADELEINE ALBRIGHT (1937-PRESENT)

LIE #4

The military is in terrible shape

"We're in greater danger today than we were the day after Pearl Harbor. Our military is absolutely incapable of defending this country."
RONALD REAGAN (1911-2004), PRESIDENTIAL CANDIDATE 1979

It started in the 1950s with the so-called "Missile Gap." The Soviets had more missiles and more warheads which put us at a dangerous disadvantage. This was the fault of the then-current Eisenhower administration. Retired Generals can always be found to verify this contention, which, of course, proved to be false after the election.

Senator John F. Kennedy started this trend which was followed by Senator Barry Goldwater in 1964 and most every other presidential candidate since then. It's always been a political winner.

Military readiness always seems to be lacking in an election year as candidates have learned that there is almost nothing that Americans respond to more strongly than their personal safety.

After the election, when the scary rhetoric has died down, it may be determined that the military was prepared for its mission after all. It can still be in the best interest of the administration to request more spending, as no politician has ever lost political capital requesting more money for the military. And so it went, all through the Cold War.

After the Iraq War, and with the continuing Afghan War and the War on Terror that may never end, it may be that our military is finally showing wear and tear of a serious nature.

Shouldn't one of the questions asked be "How do we extricate ourselves from these adventures which we cannot maintain and cannot afford?" rather than just "How much more money and manpower will it take to sustain these efforts?"

In addition to these ground, air, and drone attacks we are talking about updating our nuclear arsenal. Apparently, nuclear weapons delivered by inter-continental ballistic missile (ICBM), airplane, or submarine may need updating. The ICBMs, unused in the 72 years since Hiroshima and Nagasaki, may need an upgrade. Shouldn't we be figuring out how to eliminate or reduce these weapons, not improve them?

Since it always comes down to money, we should force our leaders to give us an option. How about a new fighter plane or bridge repair for the east coast? Increase Social Security benefits or a new aircraft carrier group? Another year in Afghanistan or the Children's Health Insurance Program (CHIP) for eight million kids? These are the options few in power talk about, but they remain very real options. Unfortunately, defense contractor lobbyists far outnumber bridge repair or children's health lobbyists and have far deeper pockets. Social Security recipients do have a powerful lobby, so they aren't going to be messed with. Now let's see who wins the votes?

"The world has nothing to fear from military ambition in our Government."
PRESIDENT JAMES K. POLK, 11TH PRESIDENT (1845-1849)

(How things have changed)

LIE #5

The National Defense budget is $700 Billion.

"Let us wage a moral and political war against war itself, so that we can cut military spending and use that money for human needs."
BERNIE SANDERS (1941-PRESENT),
SENATOR AND PRESIDENTIAL CANDIDATE 2016 AND 2020

This is untrue in a couple of ways. The announced Pentagon budget is $700 billion. This is certainly not the total defense budget. There are programs all over the place, including, but not limited to the CIA, NSA, and nuclear missiles in the Energy budget that likely bring this total to more than $1 trillion, so let's be honest about the cost.

I think we need to clarify our terms. The United States is protected on both the east and west coasts by vast oceans. To the north and to the south are friendly and far less powerful neighbors. Our border with Canada has been unguarded for more than one hundred years. No country is more favorably suited in terms of national defense.

Other than a Russian missile attack, the United States is impenetrable. If it needs to be defended at all, it can only be defended with a missile system that seems technologically unattainable at this time. We can't pour money into it, even if we wanted to. It's just not ready.

In 2016, Canada, with a similar geographic setting, spent $18.9 Billion on its defense budget.

So what are we spending a trillion dollars on? It can't be national defense. It must be national offense.

We have eleven aircraft carrier groups ready to rush to whatever hotspot there is in the world.

We have more than 800 military bases throughout the world, and that's just the known ones. We have troops all over the world, but we have men and women in harm's way in Africa chasing Islamic terrorists, in Afghanistan fighting the Taliban, in Yemen somehow involved in that civil war, in Iraq and Syria fighting ISIS and in other places we don't yet know about. (We find out when they die.)

This is in addition to 30,000 troops in Korea, thousands in Japan, and however many we have currently stationed in Europe with NATO.

None of these fine men and women are involved in national defense. They are involved in projecting American power throughout the world, but "National Defense" sounds so much better, don't you think?

A recent Air Force commercial shows a child looking up at Air Force fighters with the father exclaiming "That's the sound of freedom!" With the exception of the Axis powers in WWII, and that's a stretch, or possibly an all-out attack by the Soviets, our freedom has never been threatened from without, no matter how many potential terrorist attacks we may face. Those Air Force fighters may be making a completely different sound in other parts of the world, a sound not particularly suited to children.

> *"Every gun that is made, every warship launched, every rocket fired signifies in the final sense, a theft from those who hunger and are not fed, those who are cold and are not clothed. This world in arms is not spending money alone. It is spending the sweat of its laborers, the genius of its scientists, the hopes of its children. This is not a way of life at all in any true sense. Under the clouds of war, it is humanity hanging on a cross of iron."*
> DWIGHT D. EISENHOWER (1890-1969), PRESIDENTIAL FAREWELL SPEECH, 1961

LIE #6

Drone strikes eliminate terrorists while minimizing civilian casualties

History teaches that wars begin when governments believe the price of aggression is cheap."
PRESIDENT RONALD REAGAN - 1984 ADDRESS TO THE NATION

A recent report on America's drone program in the Middle East and Africa announced 1,264 terrorists killed in drone strikes in the last two years with only 64 civilian casualties, a ratio of approximately 20 dead terrorists for every civilian death.

A 20-1 kill ratio sounds too good to be true and is very reminiscent of the casualty reports we received during the Vietnam War. Those reports usually listed 6-20 Americans who had died, 40-60 South Vietnamese casualties, and hundreds of Viet Cong and North Vietnamese killed. Every report made it seem more and more likely that the enemy could not maintain such losses. And yet they did. It wasn't long before these reports were considered something of a joke.

Now we have a report of drones so precisely targeting terrorists that collateral damage, in the form of a civilian casualty, is a rare thing. If true, it would be a long way from past reports of mistakenly killing entire wedding parties or other gatherings, where in Afghan celebratory fashion, shots were fired into the air and the group was subsequently attacked by a drone.

In the latest report I saw there was no definition of *terrorist* or *civilian*. In the past, all males of a certain age (12? 16? 18?) were considered terrorists rather than civilians, no matter their actual status. I don't know what the metric was for this latest report. Obviously designating most males as terrorists, regardless of evidence, keeps those darn statistics in a pleasant range. A college teacher killed as a terrorist with a group of his students isn't one terrorist killed with a dozen civilian casualties, it's thirteen terrorists killed with no civilian casualties. This would just be more proof of our precision weapons and how efficiently we are managing the war.

Doesn't it seem like, after all these years, we are killing lots of terrorists without reducing the amount of terrorism? If your innocent father, mother, son, daughter, wife or husband were killed in an attack, wouldn't you possibly seek revenge and become a terrorist yourself? How about having drones shooting up houses and cars in your neighborhood, randomly and without warning? Killing a group of terrorists and civilians may actually increase the number of terrorists.

The government likes the drone program because it produces few if any direct American casualties. Americans are not particularly concerned about any casualties but their own. It can also be done quietly, without the scrutiny of the press, often from a hangar in the California desert.

We should have learned from Vietnam and other recent conflicts that the government is not always truthful when it comes to evaluating a conflict or reporting on the progress of a war. Our sudden precision in drone strikes should raise a few questions about how we are going about the "War on Terror." In the words of the great basketball coach John Wooden, "Don't mistake activity for achievement."

> *"You actually cannot sell the idea of freedom, democracy, diversity, as if it were a brand attribute and not reality -- not at the same time as you're bombing people, you can't."*
>
> NAOMI KLEIN (1970-PRESENT), ACTIVIST, AUTHOR, AND FILMMAKER.

LIE #7

We honor and respect the Military

"I have a tremendous amount of respect for military families. To have to worry about your loved ones and still try and live a normal life is extremely hard."
ASHANTI (1980-PRESENT) AMERICAN SINGER-SONGWRITER

"Liberty and democracy become unholy when their hands are dyed red with innocent blood."
MAHATMA GANDHI (1869-1948) NON-VIOLENCE IN PEACE AND WAR 1948

Vietnam was a shock to America's citizenry, a shock from which I don't think we have fully recovered. World War I, World War II and Korea were America's good wars. These wars were fought against Nazism, Fascism, and Communism; against The Kaiser, Hitler and the Commies. They were necessary wars fought by "The Greatest Generation," and we won two and tied one.

Vietnam was something else. Most Americans didn't know where it was or anything about it. We had no Vietnamese immigrants, nor did it rate a mention in the history or geography books in our schools. It was just a "police action" that morphed into a war, all sneaky like, like the damn Viet Cong.

Importantly, in 1965, most Americans would have told you their government doesn't lie. Individual politicians might lie, but not the government - and certainly not the President.

Vietnam changed all that. Our political leaders lied and our generals lied. President Johnson used some bogus shots fired at our Navy's ships to get the Gulf of Tonkin Resolution, an open-ended invitation to escalate the war. The generals proclaimed extraordinary enemy casualties as proof we were winning the war. The war, now it was a war, was being fought by draftees, mostly poor and disproportionately black who often committed horrible atrocities. Suddenly, we were no longer the good guys, and we were angry about that.

To our everlasting shame, we took out our anger on our returning troops, almost none of whom asked to go there and many came back physically and mentally wounded, if they came back at all.

Looking back on that time with guilt and shame we, as a country, decided to do better by our fighting men and women. Now no one calls them anything but "heroes" and "the brave men and women of the greatest fighting force the world has ever known." No one dare speak into a microphone to a service member or former service member without beginning with the obligatory "Thank you for your service."

But, and this is important, this is all we do. Seventeen years after 9/11 we are still in Afghanistan. We fought a war in Iraq after we went into Afghanistan, ended it, and returned home, all while we remained in Afghanistan, and returned to Iraq.

National election after election goes by without a mention of our troops over there, many of whom have served on more deployments than they can remember. Not once have we had a national discussion on the cost of all this and whether we should pay for it with a tax increase, as we did in every other war in our history.

When Osama bin Laden was killed, did we discuss whether to bring our troops home? No, we did not. After all, that's why we went there, to bring him to justice. We haven't had an honest talk about whether the war is winnable or what a win would look like.

Unlike Vietnam, there is no draft, so there is no one being dragged into a conflict in which they might die. No protests, no draft card burnings, no public funerals for the fallen. Also, no end in sight.

We salute the flag, we sing the national anthem, we thank our service men and women and we feel good about our patriotism. The words "Thank you for service" are now uttered with the frequency and same heartfelt sincerity as the grocery clerk who says "Have a good one!", whatever that means, after you purchased a quart of milk. Veterans will tell you those same people never ask "What was your service?"

Seventeen years later the war doesn't make the nightly news because there is no interest in it. There is a mention when a serviceman dies, and maybe a story if many do, but it has no staying power, perhaps because the war no longer has any purpose, or an end.

John Kerry's famous question "Who will be the last American serviceman to die for Vietnam?" is just as relevant today for Afghanistan as it was for Vietnam 50 years ago. We don't ask it today because we don't really care.

Respect and honor our military? I don't think so.

> "Innumerable soldiers have told me they don't want to be thanked for their service and they don't want to be seen as heroes (or, for that matter, villains). They want to be respected for the job they did and the pride they took in doing it well."
> ELIZABETH HEANEY "THE HONOR WAS MINE: A LOOK INSIDE THE STRUGGLES OF MILITARY VETERANS"

The Second Pillar of Democracy:
An Independent Judiciary

"I do think there is a value in the services of judges for long periods of time."
SUPREME COURT JUSTICE SONIA SOTOMAYOR (1954-PRESENT)

Our Constitution gives equal weight to the three branches of government, balancing power by not favoring one over the others. The Supreme Court's rulings are just as powerful as laws from Congress or Executive orders from the President. Supreme Court and other federal judges serve a lifetime term, theoretically removing them from politics. Beholden to no politician for their office, judges can maintain their independence. That was the intent.

The reality is that now the politics of judicial candidates are thoroughly explored before they are selected for the court. While they may change and evolve over time, their ideological starting point is well-known. Since they are lifetime appointments, younger, less experienced judges seem to be the preference now in the hope that they may influence the nation for a longer time. That eliminates many very qualified older judges, but it is what it is.

There has never been a ruling by a federal judge that has been ignored or disobeyed, though many have been severely criticized by the White House and Congress.

This check on the Executive and Legislative branches by an entrenched and lifelong serving judiciary may keep a lid on the excesses of those branches, even after an election of the same party to power in both elected branches.

In too many countries the judiciary can be intimidated or removed by a President or legislature unhappy with its rulings. This is often followed by a new Constitution giving the President greater powers, a longer term, or both.

The United States has never had such a constitutional crisis although there have been times when we were close; John Adams and the Alien and Sedition Acts in 1800, Lincoln suspending Habeus Corpus during the Civil War, FDR attempting to pack the Supreme Court when they opposed the New Deal in the 1930s, and President Nixon and Watergate in the 1970s. All followed constitutional norms, all could have gone off the rails and put us in a crisis. Maybe we've just been lucky.

SECTION II
Our Elected Officials

How did we get these guys, anyway?

"Good governance never depends upon laws, but upon the personal qualities of those who govern. The machinery of government is always subordinate to the will of those who administer that machinery. The most important element of government, therefore, is the method of choosing leaders."

FRANK HERBERT (1920-1986) – "CHILDREN OF DUNE"

LIE #8

The United States has free and fair elections

"A faith that makes losing a sin will make cheating a sacrament."
CONSERVATIVE COLUMNIST MICHAEL GERSON (1964-PRESENT)

My beautiful 5th grade teacher, Miss Clark, must have been a shill for the government. Why else would she have said "The United States, the world's oldest democracy, despite having free and fair elections, votes at a lower rate than many other of the world's democracies." She made it sound as though we were apathetic and lazy. This made fifth-grade me very sad. It turns out Miss Clark was only partially correct.

Our elections weren't free, thanks to the poll tax, and they have never been fair.

In the beginning, only white males who owned property could vote. When George Washington was elected, only 6% of Americans had the right to vote. In 1856 the vote was extended to all white men. After the Civil War came Reconstruction, giving blacks the right to vote, followed by the "Jim Crow" laws throughout the South which, through literacy tests, poll taxes, and intimidation took their voting rights away.

In 1882 the Chinese Exclusion Act passed. Guess who couldn't become citizens or vote?

In 1920 women received the right to vote, followed by Asians in 1952 and 18-year-olds in 1971.

Still, in 1924, South Carolina, which had a population of 1.6 million, elected their representatives with only 50,752 people voting, almost all of whom voted Democratic.

As we have added more voters to the rolls in our more sophisticated society, particularly women and young people ages 18-21, politicians have had to come up with more sophisticated ways to suppress the vote. These are just some of the recent tactics:

- More polling places and voting machines in favored neighborhoods, fewer in less favored places.
- Mailing inaccurate information regarding voting places and times. Moving polling places away from bus routes, college campuses, and restricting early voting days and times.
- Purging voters from the rolls if they have not voted for several elections is very popular, as is requiring Voter IDs which may be hard for opposition voters to acquire; a hunting license may be acceptable proof of identity, a college ID may not.
- Intimidation is achieved with billboards warning of the consequences of voter fraud (nearly non-existent) and the placing of police cars with sirens flashing around polling places.
- Disenfranchisement of felons removes some voters completely off the rolls.

Isn't it embarrassing to watch the TV networks show ridiculously long lines outside of polling places? Sure, it's a positive sign for turnout, but embarrassing that as the "Greatest Nation on Earth" we can't do a better job accommodating our citizens as they exercise their most basic right. Republicans have struggled for years to convince a majority of voters to embrace their ideas and vote for them, so in order to win they must suppress the vote and hope to get a plurality of those who do show up at the polls. As the party gets older and whiter, these tactics become more and more necessary. If everyone votes, Republicans rarely win, and they know it. When necessary, Democrats use similar tactics.

Most troublesome is the calculated unfairness of it all. Doesn't every school child learn about fair play growing up in the school yard?

In contrast, in India, the largest democracy in the world, there must be a polling station within two kilometers (less than two miles) of every voter.

So when Miss Clark told me Americans voted in lower numbers than other democracies, I believed her, but now I know why, and I feel better about American voters and about Miss Clark. But now I feel much worse about American politics.

As a side note, when foreign autocrats are forced to hold an election, they often hire American campaign experts to suppress the vote. After all, we're the oldest continuous democracy on the planet. We're very good at this s**t.

> *"We're like a Third World country when it comes to some of our election practices."*
> DEMOCRATIC STRATEGIST DONNA BRAZILE (1959-PRESENT)

LIE #9

One Man, One Vote.

"Pick a leader who chooses diplomacy over war. An honest broker in foreign relations. A leader with integrity, one who says what they mean, keeps their word and does not lie to their people."

AUTHOR SUZY KASSEM (1975-PRESENT)

Elbridge Gerry (with a hard G sound) was an original signer of the Declaration of Independence, a lifelong politician and diplomat, Governor of Massachusetts and Vice-President of the United States. While Governor of Massachusetts, state Senate district lines were drawn in a way favorable to his party, creating the term "gerrymandering" (soft G), to describe the geographical manipulation of districts to aid one particular party.

The phrase "partisan gerrymandering" is redundant, just like the phrase "deadly murder." Is there another kind of murder? All gerrymandering is partisan.

The net result is that even though a state may have an equal number of Democrats and Republicans, the districts may be drawn in a way that one party has a majority in many districts while the other party's voters are crammed into a few districts.

For example, Pennsylvania, a state with an equal representation of both parties' voters, has thirteen Republican House members to only five for the Democrats.

While gerrymandering has been around since almost the beginning of the Republic, it has never been as sophisticated as it is today. High tech computer modeling allows voter data to be manipulated in a way that creates grotesque looking districts that fulfill the goal of making one party sufficiently dominant to ensure victory without wasting votes on a landslide.

There are even contests to name what these districts look like, a kind of political Rorshach test. Computer modeling analyzes voting data down to the precinct level, where no vote is wasted.

In 2012, the first federal election year after redistricting following the 2010 census, Republicans received 49% of the congressional vote, yet won 13 of the 18 seats. Democrats won 51% and won 5.

Perhaps it had something to do with this map. The map looks like it was drawn by a drunk with Parkinson's disease, but it was actually drawn by a super-computer on a mission, the mission being to dilute Democratic votes as efficiently as possible, geography be damned.

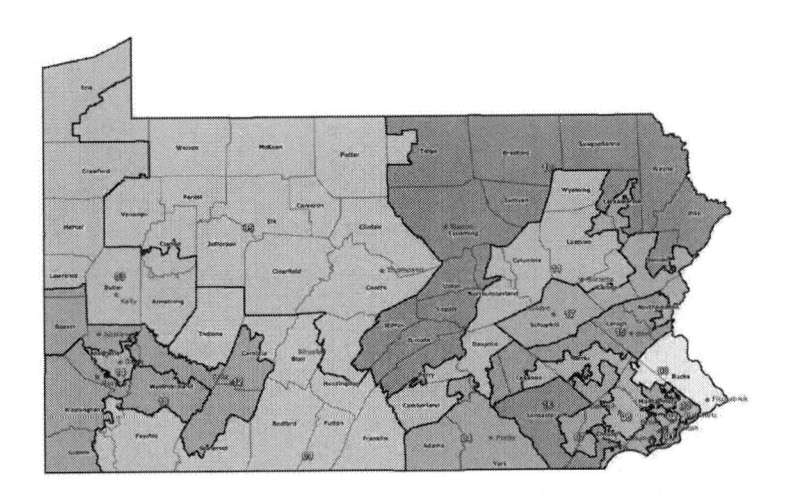

This certainly discourages voting. Fourteen of the eighteen districts were won with 60% or more of the vote. Remember, the final vote was Democrats 51%, Republican 49%, with Republicans still winning 13 of 18 seats. This is not necessarily a slam at Republicans. Democrats have done it also.

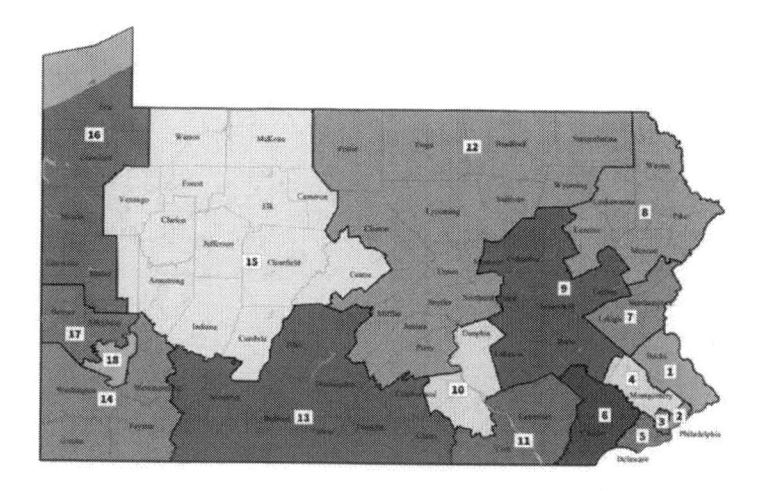

This is the new map proposed by the courts. It seems to make some sense to anyone who looks at it, and isn't that the point? Without knowing the political affiliation of the voters, this map looks like a reasonable way to apportion voters to a Congressional district. If we are to respect the fairness of the law, the law must respect us. Anyone who looks at the previous map knows that whoever came up with it was up to no good. Trying to explain the fairness of it diminishes our respect for the law.

LIE #10

One Man, One Vote, Kinda

"Free election of masters does not abolish the masters or the slaves."
PHILOSOPHER HERBERT MARCUSE (1898-1979)

I've shown you how we manipulate who gets to vote.. I've shown you how we count the votes. Now I'm going to show you how we influence who you vote for and what your elected representatives vote for.

Whatever means were used to influence the electorate back in the day - pamphlets, speeches or newspapers - the name of the game is now mass marketing, which means the name of the game is money.

It takes money to run a modern campaign and lots of it. TV, radio, internet, and social media tend to get very expensive when you have to stay in the game with your opponent. Very few elections are won by candidates who are not competitive financially. Where does that money come from? Very few constituents contribute anything. The few that do don't contribute much. That leaves the very few who contribute a lot. Who are they?

Local, city, and state races are usually funded by real estate developers of some kind. Why would they do that? They want something and usually it's more than a sympathetic ear. Often it has to do with zoning variances, tax abatements or infrastructure considerations. It's not bribery, as they often don't get their wishes, but they often do. It's been going on for a very long time so I'm sure it makes some kind of financial sense for them.

At the national level, donors tend to be corporations, unions, trade groups, or rich individuals with business before the government. They tend to donate more to one party than the other, but most hedge their bets at least somewhat.

They want similar things as the local donors: government subsidies, tax breaks, protectionism, and any other favorable perk the government can provide. Once again, the economics must work because the lobbyists and trade groups keep filling up the campaign coffers in exchange for who knows what.

While the rich often get their tax breaks and loopholes and special considerations, they get one more thing. They get the vote of their elected official. You get it also, but according to several studies, it doesn't go your way when it conflicts with the desires of the rich and powerful. You think the vote of yourself and your fellow common man commands the attention of your representative. Not very often, folks.

Almost nothing happens that the entrenched interests don't want to happen. After the Sandy Hook Elementary School massacre, 87% of the country was in favor of mandatory background checks before buying a gun. That overwhelming majority was not enough to get it passed when the gun lobby did not want it.

When oil company representatives testified before Congress, they all stated that they, as very profitable companies, no longer needed the "oil depletion allowance," a tax credit that costs the taxpayers more than $4 billion a year. It was not removed in the new tax bill, nor did many Congressional experts think it would be.

And so it goes on almost every issue. A group that studies such things found that despite what you would think, a majority of constituents wanting something almost never get it unless the top 5% want it also.

"The odd American idea that giving money to political campaigns is free speech means that the very rich have far more free speech, and so in effect far more voting power than other citizens."

TIMOTHY SNYDER (1969-PRESENT)
ON TYRANNY: 20 LESSONS FROM THE 20TH CENTURY

Intermission
Phrases that Lie

"Language is not only the vehicle of thought, it is a great and efficient instrument in thinking."

SIR HUMPHREY DAVY (1778-1829) CHEMIST

I told a friend this chapter was titled "Phrases that Lie" and she said, "Oh, you mean euphemisms." The dictionary definition of "euphemism" is "a mild or indirect word or expression substituted for one considered to be too harsh or blunt." I said "No, I mean words that lie." Euphemisms disguise unpleasantness. Lying words hide real pain and harm. The words and phrases that follow have been used to circumvent laws and regulations and have caused real damage to our democracy. Many still insist on using them. Let's start with the heavy hitters.

Enemy Combatant – Dick Cheney and George W. Bush needed a phrase to describe all the unfortunate souls caught up in our Afghanistan dragnet that would keep them from being protected by the Geneva Convention of 1949, which set the humanitarian standards for war. Prisoners of War (remember the "War on Terror?") would have been protected by international standards, enemy combatants are not. Without protections they could be held indefinitely (remember Guantanamo?) and be subjected to …

Enhanced Interrogation Techniques – Full credit to the guy who came up with this phrase. This is nothing but torture, even though the government insisted that torture had to be something which caused organ failure or death. Once again, I say "Really!" Extreme cold, stress positions for hours on end, blinding light, deafening rock music and sleep deprivation apparently don't qualify. They do for me and they should for you, unless you dig that sort of thing. And let's not forget everyone's favorite – waterboarding, which does not "simulate" drowning but is actual drowning. Japanese prison guards were executed for waterboarding U.S. prisoners in WWII, but for us it's just an "enhanced interrogation technique."

Extraordinary Rendition – Once again, a very clever phrase, which simply means kidnapping from a foreign country and transporting to another foreign country. We know about this practice because the Italians took offense when in 2003 a Muslim cleric, Abu Omar, was snatched from the streets of Milan and transported to Egypt for interrogation. They have excellent "interrogators" in Egypt. Twenty-three CIA officers were indicted and convicted of kidnapping, although none were at the trial or ever plan to be in Italy again and we're never going to let them be extradited back to Milan.

Turkey has their eyes on a cleric in Pennsylvania that they'd like to extract, er, I mean conduct an "extraordinary rendition". Imagine how we would feel about that.

Collateral Damage – I think we all know this means civilian casualties, particularly those we did not intend to kill. It makes kill and casualties almost sound civilized, even excusable.

Overseas contingency operations – Secret military strikes, often unauthorized by Congress

We now move to Finance where it wasn't until 2008 and the world collapsed that we'd even heard of these terms, unfortunately.

Collateralized Debt Obligation (CDO) – I've read the definition several times and still don't understand it, just as it was designed to do. A CDO is a bunch of mortgages, worthless or otherwise, sliced up and repackaged, called a mortgage bond and sold like any other bond, except the underlying assets are practically unknown, although all were rated AAA. No chance for Wall Street mischief there.

Unfortunately, thousands of ordinary people had their life savings invested in these assets, recommended by people who should have known better – bankers, brokers, and investment advisers. For these ordinary souls, it did not go well.

Tranche – That's French for slice, as in your mortgage is cut up into different "tranches" in your "CDO." Couldn't use "slice?" You know they are getting tricky when they use French!

Credit Default Swap – Insurance on your CDO. In a nutshell, the CDOs, thought to be rock solid by those who had them (they weren't), were insured many times over. Imagine everyone on your street having fire insurance on your wooden house. This is not going to end well.

Carried interest – Originally used by explorers sent on overseas trading expeditions, the term was resurrected for hedge fund managers to obfuscate (like that word? It means to make unclear or unintelligible) why they were paying capital gains rates without investing any capital. A tax loophole for a select group of wealthy individuals it changed their tax rate from 39% to 15%. It was supposed to be eliminated in the new tax bill. It was not.

Too Big to Fail – There is no lie here. This is the description of the banks involved in the financial shenanigans above, all of whom survived and shortly prospered, thanks to a government bailout. Homeowners were not so lucky.

Too Big to Jail – The CEOs and Vice-presidents of these "too big to fail" banks were deemed "too big to jail." No one has properly explained this.

SECTION III
Money, Money, Money

"Through tattered clothes great vices do appear; Robes and furred gowns hide all. Plate sin with gold and the strong lance of justice hurtless breaks. Arm it in rags, a pigmy's straw doth pierce it."

WILLIAM SHAKESPEARE, KING LEAR *

Shakespeare is saying, in other words, "The rich are bulletproof!"

LIE #11

Congress swears an oath to defend the Constitution and to the Constitution alone.

"I don't want to do away with government. I just want to reduce it to the size where I can put it in the bathtub and drown it."
GROVER NORQUIST (1956-PRESENT), CREATOR OF
"AMERICANS FOR TAX REFORM"

This statement is only partially a lie. Congress swears an oath to the Constitution, but Republicans also sign a pledge to "Americans for Tax Reform", a pledge they seem to take as seriously as their oath to the Constitution. This pledge promises not to vote for any tax increases of any kind, for any circumstances.

You see, it says on their website that Ronald Reagan himself asked Grover Norquist to start this group. Really? As with so many organizations in Washington, the name is misleading. "Americans for Tax Reform" is not interested in tax reform. They care about one thing, and one thing only – reducing taxes.

Under threat of a primary challenge, and with lots of money for that challenge, Mr. Norquist has every Republican legislative prospect or incumbent sign a pledge stating that he/she will not vote for any new taxes or any tax increases. None, nada, zilch.

The most notable incident of someone breaking away from this pledge was President George H.W. Bush who famously pronounced at his nominating convention "Read my lips. NO new taxes." He later signed a bill authorizing a tax increase when it seemed to be the right thing to do for the country. We all know how that turned out. President Bush was denied a second term by Bill Clinton, Ross Perot, and a Republican Party obsessed with taxes.

No one has stepped out of line since. This has created some odd government conversations, or non-conversations.

The Federal Highway tax is a good example. In 1997 the Federal Highway fuel tax was 18.4 cents per gallon. In the 20 years since then we have put more cars on the highway but with much better fuel economy and road repairs have gotten more expensive.

This has created a deficit in the Highway Trust Fund used for repairs; $8 billion in 2008, $7 billion in 2009 and nearly $20 billion in 2010. The only legislative initiatives have been to eliminate the tax for short periods of time, but they have not succeeded. There has been absolutely no public discussion of raising the tax to cover necessary road and bridge repairs, despite the shortfalls to the trust fund and the stability of gas prices, making a gas tax hike relatively painless. This is totally irresponsible.
If a tax increase so obvious and necessary is not on the table, what is? Private roads?

America's infrastructure isn't threadbare because the country is poor. It's threadbare because the country became cheap when it came to asking those with the most resources to spend something close to what citizens of other countries spend on common goods.

This mentality now permeates the Republican delegation to Congress. When Republicans control the House of Representatives, where all tax bills must originate, there is absolutely no tax discussion whatsoever, except possibly a tax cut, even when the government is running a massive deficit and the economy is doing fine. Budgets keep expanding due to inflation, and with no new revenue, so do deficits. And yet we just passed a $150 billion a year tax cut, without reducing spending. Mommy, Mommy, make them stop.

LIE #12

Attack Waste, Fraud and Abuse to Reduce the Budget Deficit

"It is a popular delusion that the government wastes vast amounts of money through inefficiency and sloth. Enormous effort and elaborate planning are required to waste this much money."

P.J. O'ROURKE (1947-PRESENT), PARLIAMENT OF WHORES: A LONE HUMORIST ATTEMPTS TO EXPLAIN THE ENTIRE U.S. GOVERNMENT

I long for the days when the budget deficit was small enough that it could almost plausibly be claimed that these three gremlins, waste, fraud, and abuse, if managed, could balance the budget.

Of course, those were the days of $100 billion deficits, not $600 billion plus like today. They were also the days of the Pentagon's $500 hammers and $1000 toilet seats. Younger readers may not remember those, but they got quite a lot of press in their day.

Waste, Fraud, and Abuse were equal opportunity scoundrels. Democrats and Republicans both found them very helpful in any election campaign. The Pentagon was the favorite target, but all government agencies were fair game.

Nowadays it takes a "60 Minutes" expose' on some weapons system, or an outrageous no-bid contract to make news, like the $300 million deal a two-man firm from Montana got for the electrification of Puerto Rico . If the agency accounting departments had more auditors, they could keep a closer eye on alleged cost overruns, overpayments, undocumented expenses and whatever other tricks were being used to increase their share of the taxpayers' trillions. For instance, as of 2013, there were 4,300 auditors at the Defense Contract Audit Agency (DCAA). Double that number and billions would be saved.

However, a simple Wikipedia search of the DCAA shows how an agency can be corrupted by large corporate interests with large political donations. Failing grades overruled by managers, passing grades given with little or no documentation, and harassment of auditors by managers wishing to overturn unfavorable audits are just some of what was discovered by investigations. A 2009 report on the agency found "an environment not conducive to producing quality audits." Who benefits from such an environment? Not the public. The defense contractors? Maybe.

Even as politicians clamor for more oversight regarding these three villains, they never want to pay for it. There were never enough auditors overseeing those multi-billion dollar defense contracts. Now it's just a employment revolving door between government employees, including legislators, and defense contractors.

Big defense contractors with large lobbying staffs and rich campaign coffers do not like quality audits and they have the clout to interfere with the process. Since competent auditors are worth hundreds of multiples of their salaries, corrupting them is considered "Money Well Spent."

IRS audits are down also. No one likes the IRS, but the fear of an audit is what keeps many of us honest and lets us believe that our neighbor is also. It's what makes voluntary compliance successful and efficient. The U.S. spends about 60 cents per $100 in collections. If people perceive the system is unfair (there's that word again!) compliance rates will drop.
The IRS budget has been cut once again, reducing auditors and audits, reducing tax revenues. This makes no fiscal sense, but it does make political sense as large campaign contributors are among those most likely to be audited. How much can you save as a multi-millionaire

with a shaky tax shelter if you don't get audited? "Campaign donations well spent."

The lack of political advantage by crying waste, fraud, and abuse leads me to believe that the large corporate government contractors have won the day. Waste, fraud and abuse were never the budget criminals politicians made them out to be, but they were villains all the same that needed a constant watchdog. That watchdog has become old and toothless. Instead of being the junkyard dog viciously tugging at his chain to attack anyone threatening the public purse, he seems to be curled up asleep at the fireplace as the burglar waltzes in and ransacks the place. This Congressional silence suggests a truce between those who would protect taxpayer dollars and those who would fill their pockets at the public expense.

Congressman Billy Tauzin from Louisiana shepherded the Medicare Prescription Drug bill through Congress and promptly retired to become head of the pharmaceutical association responsible for lobbying the Congress. Coincidentally, that bill had a clause that prohibited Medicare from negotiating drug prices. Can't get much more obvious than that.

> "The rich control our politics to a huge extent. In return they get tax cuts and deregulation. It's been, and is, an amazing ride for the rich."
> JEFFREY SACHS (1954-PRESENT) ECONOMIST

LIE #13

Americans are overtaxed

"Those who wish to reap the benefits of this great nation must bear the fatigue of supporting it."

THOMAS PAINE (1737-1809), AUTHOR OF "COMMON SENSE,"
THE PAMPHLET MOST RESPONSIBLE FOR SWAYING POPULAR SUPPORT
FOR THE AMERICAN REVOLUTION

The American Conservative movement became prominent with the Presidential nomination of Barry Goldwater in 1964. One of the pillars of the movement is low taxation because "people know better than the government how to spend their money." Since the election of Ronald Reagan in 1980, "Americans' taxes are too high" has been burned into the American psyche.

Republicans and Democrats are loath to raise taxes. Republicans, as was noted earlier, have pledged to never raise taxes, leaving Democrats as the only party willing to discuss a tax increase. This does not go down well politically.

It does not matter that Americans, when compared to other prosperous nations, rank fourth from the bottom in levels of taxation, above only Ireland, Chile and Mexico.

It does not matter that the United States has a glaring infrastructure problem evident to anyone who travels to Europe or the Far East.

It does not matter that the U.S. has a budget deficit of more than $500 billion.

And finally, it does not matter that the rich and super-rich have managed to keep their taxes at historically low levels.

In 1992 Mitt Romney ran for the Senate in Massachusetts against incumbent Edward (Ted) Kennedy. Romney attacked Kennedy for his refusal to show his tax returns. In 2012 Romney, after working for years for Bain Capital, a private equity fund where he made a bundle, ran for President against Barack Obama. He was willing to supply two years of tax returns, years where he knew he was running for President and filed knowing they would be public - but nothing from prior years.

Ted Kennedy with his inherited wealth, and Mitt Romney with his Wall Street wealth, both risked losing an important election rather than reveal their tax returns. This can only mean the income was ridiculously large, the taxes ridiculously small, or both.

The Tax Reform Act of 1986, negotiated by Republican President Ronald Reagan and Democratic House Speaker Tip O'Neill, significantly reformed the American tax system. It lowered the top tax bracket from 50% to 28%, after the 1981 tax cut had already lowered it from 70% to 50%. It raised the bottom rate from 11% to 15% and raised the Capital gains rate to the ordinary income rate. Also during the Reagan years estate taxes were considerably lowered.

There are three important points here. One is that the rich did very well during the Reagan years. The second is that since 1986, the year the tax code was "fixed," there have been 30,000 changes to the tax code, almost all of which are unknown and irrelevant to me and you, but very important to someone. A change in a line here, or a phrase there may have benefited a group or individual millions of dollars in tax savings. 30,000 changes in 30 years is three changes every single day. Now you know why the tax code is 2,600 pages.

Thirdly, the government collects about $3.3 trillion in taxes. It gives out tax credits equal to a third of that amount. If the government wishes to subsidize something it should do so, not hide the subsidy in a tax credit. All these adjustments rarely help the guy who works for a paycheck, which is perhaps why we feel that we are overtaxed.

LIE #14

The "Death Tax" hurts farmers and small business

Here are two opposing opinions on the death of inheritance taxes

"And after generations of redistributive progressive income and inheritance taxes, the economic elite was losing its lead. Income in America during the mid-1970s was as equally distributed as at any time in the country's history."
JANE MAYER (1955-PRESENT), "DARK MONEY"

"I think not having the estate tax recognizes the people that are investing... as opposed to those that are just spending every darn penny they have, whether it's on booze or women or movies."
SENATOR CHARLES GRASSLEY (1933-PRESENT) (R) IOWA

The Rockefellers, the Vanderbilts and the Kennedys are familiar American names notable for their long-time wealth. John D. Rockefeller made a fortune in the oil business, Cornelius Vanderbilt made his in railroads, and Joe Kennedy in bootlegging, all during the early part of the last century. While the families are still synonymous with great wealth, none of them seems to have advanced the family business, or any other business, for the last 100 years; yet they remain fabulously wealthy despite the inheritance taxes in effect through the years.

The richest Americans amassed huge fortunes, passed them on to their heirs and created a new aristocracy. Their ranks swell every year as families like the Waltons of Wal-Mart fame, casino magnate Sheldon Adelson, Dianne Hendricks in building supplies and a slew of hedge fund managers join the club. These are the fortunes estate taxes were designed for. Unfortunately, these are the fortunes they too often miss. Currently the tax is assessed only on estates exceeding $5.3 million or $10.6 million for a married couple. This applies to 1 out of 700 deaths in the U.S. Most rich families find the loopholes that make a top rate of 40% turn into an effective rate of 17%, with much of the estate totally protected from the tax. Families like the Rockefellers, Vanderbilts, Waltons, and Adelsons have exploited loopholes in the tax to avoid paying $billions.

Republicans, according to Leo McGarry of "The West Wing" drama, are very good at naming things. The "Death Tax" is an excellent name for a tax you oppose. It's not a death tax. It's a wealth tax.

Only about 20 family farms or small businesses are affected by the tax every year, with virtually none of them having to be sold to pay the tax. I'm not sure those that have to sell would be considered "small" by the average taxpayer.

In 2014 the estate tax raised $19.3 billion, or .6% of government revenue. It was projected to raise $225 billion over 10 years. The Republicans in Congress have a bill to repeal the estate tax with no alternative to replace the lost revenue.

Some, maybe many, perhaps most Americans believe, in principle, that money earned and taxed in your lifetime should pass freely to your heirs. I understand their feelings. For most, that is exactly what happens, but unless we want a permanent class of wealthy families, an estate tax is essential to any attempt to level the playing field for all Americans.

Besides, we need the money. We now have astronomical budget deficits alongside needs we cannot afford to meet. For the same reason Willy Sutton robbed banks (that's where the money is!), we need to tax the rich, and especially the super-rich. Whether it is through income taxes or estate taxes is just a matter of policy.

Modern economies have a way of creating fewer winners than in the past, but those winners take a larger and larger share of the profits. Facebook won the battle for social media. No one is getting rich from

AOL or MySpace. Amazon's domination of e-commerce only seems to grow. Microsoft dominates computer operating systems with Apple a very distant runner-up. These companies and others that dominate their industries create great fortunes which don't "trickle down" to the average working man as Reaganomics would have had you believe.

Bill Gates or Mark Zuckerburg couldn't possibly spend $200 million in their lifetimes, yet they own hundreds of times that. This cannot be good for the economy or for the hardworking men and women of America.

"Once you realize that trickle-down economics does not work, you will see the excessive tax cuts for the rich as what they are – a simple upward redistribution of income, rather than a way to make all of us richer, as we were told."
HA-JOON CHANG AUTHOR, "23 THINGS THEY DON'T TELL YOU ABOUT CAPITALISM"

LIE #15

A Corporation's only duty is to Shareholder Value

"The social responsibility of business is to increase its profits."
MILTON FRIEDMAN (1912-2006) GODFATHER OF
THE CHICAGO SCHOOL OF ECONOMICS

Milton Friedman, legendary Republican free market economist stated the above quote in 1979 at the beginning of the Reagan Revolution. It has been gospel in many circles since then.

Traditionally, corporate responsibilities were threefold:
- Increase shareholder value
- Protect worker interests
- Be a good "citizen" of the community

Typically, this meant profits for the corporation, steady employment for the workers and consideration for the community, whether it was in regards to environmental concerns, community charities or local government.

Friedman felt that only the shareholders should be considered. All else would take care of itself if business stuck to the business of creating value for shareholders. Let's see how that's worked out.

From 2003-2013 the 449 publicly traded companies on the S&P 500 spent 54% of revenues on stock buybacks, 37% on dividends and the remaining 9% on investment and employee wage increases. Not really what we were looking for.

This is neither good for growth nor for employees.

A locally owned business has to make a profit to stay in business, but maximizing that profit is not the only consideration when making business decisions.

The owner lives in the community where his business is located. His kids go to the local school, he and his wife have friends who work in the business. If it's a large business, the town relies on it for tax revenue.

If the owner who makes a 10% profit on his investment has the chance to make a 15% profit by moving the business overseas, maximizing shareholder profit is not the only consideration. Other factors may outweigh the increase in profits. For instance, after firing all your friends and devastating the town, you might have to move; quickly.

As the ownership of a corporation moves further away geographically, other considerations than profit become less important. Environmental considerations become less important as decision makers do not live with the consequences of those decisions. Often the death knell for a company and town occurs when the company is sold to out of town interests.

Mr. Friedman suggests that this is all just part of the "creative destruction" that is capitalism, as if it were simple to recreate those jobs and tax revenue to replace that which is lost.

When shareholder value becomes the only consideration, it may be time to reconsider what value corporations bring to the economy, and whether the rules should be changed.

Corporate personhood is the concept that corporations have some of the same rights as people, as described in several Supreme Court decisions through the years. Perhaps those rights should be reconsidered since corporate citizenship has become less valuable to the community.

"If corporations are people, they're not the kind of people you'd want to take home to meet your parents. Imagine a person who is totally self-absorbed, greedy, phony, amoral at best, and downright immoral at worst. And if that's not bad enough, corporate "people" are also rich, immune from physical injury, and for all practical purposes, immortal."

DAVID NIOSE, (1962-PRESENT) " FIGHTING BACK THE RIGHT; RECLAIMING AMERICA FROM THE ATTACK ON REASON"

LIE #16

The Poor are Poor due to bad choices

"Hope is a good thing, maybe the best thing."
ANDY DUFRESNE IN "THE SHAWSHANK REDEMPTION," 1994 MOVIE

In their book "Poor Economics: A Radical Rethinking of the Way to Fight Global Poverty," which I highly recommend for its information, insights and readability, Abhijit V. Banerjee and Esther Duflo examine the 865 million people who live on $1 a day and how to help them.

First, you need to understand them. From their foreword:

> "What is striking is that even people who are that poor are just like the rest of us in almost every way. We have the same desires and weaknesses; the poor are no less rational than anyone else-quite the contrary. Precisely because they have so little, we find them putting much careful thought into their choices: they have to be sophisticated economists just to survive. Yet our lives are as different as liquor and liquorice."

> "It means living in a world whose institutions are not built for you."

We like to think of the poor as poor for a reason; unfortunately, we often disagree on the reasons. Liberals cite poor nutrition, poor education, and poor neighborhood environment. Conservatives cite poor family structure (read single parent), poor work habits, and no ambition due to government handouts.

I'm sure there is some truth in all these reasons, but that's not what we are going to talk about. While people living on $1 a day are not the same as America's poor, there are similarities.

Just because you don't understand the decisions of the poor, does not mean those decisions are not rational. Throughout their book Banerjee and Duflo talk about the poor and their problems. Their method was the scientific method: they saw a problem, created a solution, implemented it, and watched what happened. Guess what? It often didn't work, but our intrepid authors didn't just throw up their hands and complain about the stupid people they were working with. They asked "Why didn't it work?" With greater understanding came better solutions which often did work. Often politicians give up too easily due to political opposition, when they only needed a slightly different solution. Venture capitalists know that 80-90% of their projects will fail and yet they continue, hoping that the 10-20% that succeed will make them rich. Taxpayer money invested in failed projects is always a political disaster, no matter how much you learned or how much closer you have come to solving the problem. Unfortunately, there usually are no second chances, no opportunities to improve. Wouldn't it make more sense to take the long view, start small and admit that we won't get it perfectly right the first time? But that's not how politics and government work. It is certainly not how politics works in our highly partisan environment where every failure is a sledgehammer to use against those in power.

Lyndon Johnson's "War on Poverty" is a conservative's example of failed government policy because it did not eliminate poverty. Total victory seems like an impossibly high bar for such an intractable problem, especially in a time period not measured in generations. What war have we been in lately that did have total victory? I rest my case.

The initiatives begun by President Johnson: Medicare, Medicaid, Food Stamps, Head Start and VISTA significantly lowered poverty rates in the United States. From 1964, when the programs began, poverty dropped from 17.3% to 11.1% by 1973. It has remained between 11% and 16% ever since.

Perceived as programs to alleviate black poverty, Johnson's programs fell out of favor in the 1970s as the economy slowed. I repeat, this does not make this a failure, just not a total victory. As is often the case, the resources needed to win this war may have been underestimated, as was the will of the people to sustain it.

A perceived U.S. problem today is the use of PayDay lenders; check cashing services that charge ridiculously high interest rates. Why would anyone use them rather than a bank? Well, most banks require minimum deposits to open an account and charge fees for low balances and branches are often not located in poor neighborhoods. Ohh! Did I mention that my kid has an earache and I have no money for the medicine?

That is what it's like living in a world "whose institutions are not created for you."

In poor countries, the goal for most of the very poor or their children was to get a government job. Before you conservatives jump with glee and start doing the latest Republican dance (the Hokey-pokey?) let me explain. For most of these people, the clerk at the courthouse or a nurse at the clinic was the only steady employment in the village. Nothing, I repeat *Nothing* makes a family more hopeful than a steady paycheck. It allows one to think of the future, to plan for the future. Without it, life is just an everyday struggle. It's not the government job that is so attractive. It's the job security.

Think about that every time you hear that the unemployment rate is "only" 6.5% or that there are one, two or three million people unemployed for a year or more. Where is their hope?

My brother had a landscaping business that earned about $40,000 a year. His income was heavily weighted to the warm weather months: $20,000 in the spring, 15,000 in the summer, $5,000 in the fall, $0 in the winter. He claimed he made less than I did because I made $10,000 every season, for a total of $40,000. Was he right?

Now ask yourself this? How would you react to these situations when finances were tight: the last time you got a bonus check, or had a big paycheck due to overtime, or had a good sale? Would you be more or less likely to go out for dinner, give in to your child's wishes, or buy yourself a new something? I thought so. If you can, imagine you are very poor. What do you think it would feel like to have a few dollars in your pocket or to buy something nice for your family? These are not easy temptations to resist. Often saving for a future goal gets derailed for immediate needs. If that happens repeatedly, instant gratification may replace that future goal - it just will!

In third world countries, high school education for girls went up when they changed the due date for tuition until after the harvest rather than just a few weeks earlier. Simple idea. Just tweaking the tuition date went a very long way in solving the higher education problem for girls. Instead of blaming the poor for their poverty, perhaps we could better understand their situation and how to improve it. The social science is out there, we just need to be more patient with the remedies.

"Poverty doesn't give you strength or teach you lessons about perseverance. No, poverty only teaches you how to be poor
SHERMAN ALEXIE (1966-PRESENT) "THE ABSOLUTELY TRUE DIARY OF A PART-TIME INDIAN"

LIE #17

Income Inequality is a feature of U.S. Capitalism

"When plunder becomes a way of life for a group of men in a society, over the course of time they create for themselves a legal system that authorizes it and a moral code that glorifies it."
FREDERIC BASTIAT(1801-1850)-FRENCH ECONOMIST

The year 1970 saw a string of 41 straight years where middle-class incomes grew faster than upper-class incomes. In 1929, the top 1% had 24% of all income; in 1970 it was 9%. By 2007 it was back up to 24%. Meanwhile, the bottom 90% went from sharing 52% of income in 1928 to 68% in 1970 to the year 2012, where it was 49%, the first time it had ever dipped below half.

As income inequality fell after WWII, the economy remained strong, putting the lie to the fact that inequality must be a consequence of our high risk, high reward economy. The real income on federal tax returns by the vast majority of Americans, the 90%, doubled between the end of WWII and 1973.

Beginning in the 1970s, America transformed from a place where they make things to one where new financial instruments and deals were the ticket to wealth, and income inequality began to rise. This can't be coincidence.

Also in the 1970s, the rich began fighting unionization, since fighting was cheaper than obeying the law. This, along with more industry moving to the less labor friendly South, killed the unions. This was also the end of management sharing the wealth with the workers. This comes as no surprise, since they didn't willingly share the wealth with workers before unions.

Through campaign contributions, the rich controlled our politics, receiving tax cuts and deregulation, which only made them richer.

As stated earlier, companies have spent more and more of their earnings on stock buybacks and dividends, and less on wages, increasing inequality.

Globalization has contributed to this trend in several ways. Workers, afraid of losing their jobs to cheaper labor overseas, were much more willing to accept stagnant wages.

Profits from the sale of cheaper overseas goods flowed to the top, often devastating local industries. The liberal trade policies that produced this wealth and carnage never saw fit to retrain or reinvigorate those who suffered from these policies.

According to David Cay Johnston in <u>Divided: The Perils of Our Growing Inequality</u>, "We have created a society in which all the nation's economic gains flow to the top and the vast majority see income stagnation or decline. We have embraced bankruptcy, debt, long bouts of joblessness, and flat or shrinking paychecks as the new normal. And we have lavished cash, tax cuts, and subtle subsidies on the richest among us, whose prosperity continues to blossom."

Today, the top 25 hedge fund managers earn more than all the kindergarten teachers in America, and pay only 15% in taxes.

"The test of our progress is not whether we add more to the abundance of those who have much, it is whether we provide for those who have little."
FRANKLIN D. ROOSEVELT (1882-1945) 32ND PRESIDENT

The Third Pillar of Democracy:
Innovation and Entrepreneurship

"The French don't even have a word for entrepreneur."
GEORGE W. BUSH (1946-PRESENT) 43RD PRESIDENT

The U.S. is not the only country to cultivate innovation and entrepreneurship, but we seem to be very good at it, perhaps the best. With 377 Nobel prizes awarded, the U.S. has more than the next five countries combined. While many of those were awarded for basic science, the U.S. has also been very good at turning the breakthroughs of basic science into useful, everyday products that have made life on this planet just a little bit easier.

Men like Alexander Graham Bell, Nikola Tesla, Thomas Edison and other entrepreneurs that followed have built the U.S. economy into the largest in the world.

The U.S. government supports basic research, often through grants to an excellent university system, and then makes that research available to the private sector. The successes of this research are often preceded by many, many failures; failures which the private sector would be unwilling to fund.

The military, in the never-ending race for superiority, is often the source of successful research. In the '60s, Tang, a breakfast drink invented by NASA for the Apollo astronauts, was heavily advertised as a moon-race spinoff. The Apollo moon project had many other achievements of even more significance, including special cooling and heat-resistant fabrics, solar cells, pacemakers and other medical devices, cordless-tool technology and many, many others.

In the '90s, the Defense Advanced Research Project Agency (DARPA) gave us the "Internet." Advanced computing power made it what it is today. The Internet may have the longer-lasting and greater impact, but Tang was quite tasty.

Wall Street and its access to capital, and America's favorable business climate, including its bankruptcy regulations, has made the formation of new businesses far easier than in most places around the globe. These businesses have helped keep the American economy foremost among the economies of the world, as small businesses are the ones to take advantage of new technologies and are the source of most innovation and new employment.

When times become more difficult, democracies may struggle. People look for new solutions in difficult circumstances, often turning to someone who claims that they have the answer to their problems.

Most who remembered the "Great Depression" and the political and social turmoil it created are dead now. Democracy was only one of several political systems vying for dominance. Communism, Socialism, and Fascism all had their adherents, and Democracy was not a sure thing to remain our political system. If World War II had not come along, and with it the war effort that put everyone to work, we may have changed the Republic in ways that we can't even imagine today.

Economic well-being is a necessity to preserving a democratic system. As we confront income inequality, poverty, and economic uncertainty, it's important to keep in mind how fragile our democratic system truly is. Innovation and entrepreneurship make it just a little bit stronger.

SECTION IV
Government

"...I do not believe that the power and duty of the General Government ought to be extended to the relief of individual suffering....the lesson should be constantly enforced that, though the people support the Government, the Government should not support the people."
GROVER CLEVELAND, 22ND PRESIDENT, IN 1887
AFTER VETOING A RELIEF BILL FOR TEXAS FARMERS

I can conceive of no better service in the United States, henceforth, by democrats of thorough and heart-felt faith, than boldly exposing the weakness, liabilities and infinite corruptions of democracy.
WALT WHITMAN-19TH CENTURY POET

LIE #18

U.S. Finance Leads the World Economy

"And they saw that praise was reserved henceforth for those who devised means of getting paid enormously for committing crimes against which no laws had been passed....Thus the American dream turned belly up.
KURT VONNEGUT(1922-20007) - "GOD BLESS YOU, MR. ROSEWATER"

In the early years of American history, raw materials were the source of America's wealth. First furs, then tobacco, then rice and grain were exported. Cotton became by far the most valuable export crop of the first half of the 19th century. By the beginning of the 20th century, manufactured goods based on iron and steel were leading the way. By the end of the century it was creative and technology- driven products that were most important.

One consistent part of all this growth was finance. Capital was needed to grow these enterprises and the banks were there to lend it. However, through most of our history, finance was the grease that moved the economy and was a relatively small proportion of that economy. Now finance is estimated to be as much as 30% of the U.S. economy.

This is a problem. Banks do not produce any goods, and while raising capital for business is important, it's not 30% important. What else do they do? They speculate on the stock market. Terms like "credit default swaps" and "derivatives" were unknown before the 2008 financial meltdown; now they swirl around on the talk shows like they've always been part of American lingo.

Large banks that were "too big to fail" gambled knowing that the nation could not afford to let them go bankrupt. Since we could not, we did not. But, we supposedly learned from this mistake.

The Dodd-Frank financial bill, which barely passed, and had large Republican opposition, was going to fix all that. Unfortunately, many parts of the law were formed or written by bank lobbyists. This can't be good for the American people. Banks that were too big to fail have gotten bigger. Talk of their breakup is nowhere to be found.

I recently saw an ad for Goldman-Sachs, the largest investment bank of Wall Street. It explained how a particular successful small business could not have expanded without the capital Goldman raised and all those new jobs would not have been created. Yes, but this is now small potatoes for banks like Goldman-Sachs. The real money is elsewhere. The Dodd-Frank bill had a provision that stocks had to be held for a certain period of time. The banks went nuts and did everything in their power to get this provision removed. They eventually succeeded. The time frame they objected to: 90 days? No. 30 days? No. 7 days? No. One day? No. The time frame was, are you ready, one second. What kind of "investment" bank objects to holding a stock for one second? The speculating kind, of course. And that's what the big banks on Wall Street are, and we are doing nothing about it until the next big crash.

Dodd-Frank created the Consumer Financial Protection Bureau (CFPB) to aid consumers in their dealings with financial institutions. It was supposed to help in everything from mortgages, credit cards, payday lenders, student loans and more. The banks hate it, and have tried to gut it, and Republicans have helped them in this effort.

The recent Wells Fargo scandal, where Wells Fargo created 3.5 million extra accounts for people without their knowledge, was uncovered and prosecuted by the CFPB. So far they have recovered, through repayments and fines, billions of dollars. This is only the beginning and that's why the banks fear it.

> *"We've indulged in this fiction that we can build a vibrant economy by deregulating the financial sector, and cutting taxes and putting off investing in infrastructure and education. But we can't anymore. And now we have to ask the question about what really went wrong. Because without the right story about what really went wrong, we won't fix what needs to be fixed.*
> SENATOR AND 2020 PRESIDENTIAL CANDIDATE ELIZABETH WARREN (1949-PRESENT) (D) MASS.

LIE #19

Business is drowning in Burdensome Regulation

"He was in danger? Yes. Grave danger? Is there any other kind?"
COURTROOM SCENE IN "A FEW GOOD MEN" 1992 MOVIE

When business talks about regulation the word most commonly used is "burdensome." While I'm sure each and every regulation adds some additional cost in money or time to a business, I don't believe they all rise to the distinction of "burdensome."

Many regulations are reporting requirements that involve a one-time adjustment and an additional line on a form. Others surely qualify as "burdensome," but for what reason?

Business generally hates regulation as it cuts into profits, but we have seen what unregulated or poorly regulated businesses are capable of. The Upper Big Branch mine in West Virginia exploded due to poor ventilation, killing twenty-eight miners, because the blowers, an expense, were turned off. Volkswagen couldn't make their diesel engines perform to EPA emission standards so they had their engineers readjust the onboard computers to fool the EPA emissions testing equipment. The Deepwater Horizon offshore drilling rig of British Petroleum (BP) blew up, killing 12 workers and causing the Gulf of Mexico's greatest environmental disaster ever. Ignoring safety regulations was determined to be a primary cause of the explosion.

All these industries have government inspectors overseeing their activities, but they are ridiculously understaffed with limited enforcement power.

BP paid out billions in fines and clean up costs. Volkswagen was fined heavily and had to recall millions of vehicles. Don Blankenship, owner of Massey Energy, owner of Upper Big Branch mine went to jail for a year and had significant financial penalties. Notably, he was the only one to face criminal penalties in all these scandals. The others treated the fines from their illegal activities as a cost of doing business.

Wouldn't it be nice if we didn't have to worry about all these regulations? We could go about our business without worrying about worker safety or damage to the environment. You may think that most companies would act responsibly but history has shown that far too many do not. Without fear of financial penalty even more would act irresponsibly.

Of course there can be over-regulation just as there can be under-regulation, but how many additional swindles, accidents, and schemes would have been perpetrated on the American people without proper regulation and enforcement?

With the current mood for deregulation, I fear we may find out.

> *"Deregulation is a transfer of power from the trodden to the treading. It is unsurprising that all conservative parties claim to hate big government."*
> FRENCH ESSAYIST GEORGE MONBIOT (1963-PRESENT)

LIE #20

States' Rights counterbalance an ever increasing Federal government.

"The truth that survives is simply the lie that is pleasantest to believe."
H.L.MENCKEN-1920S NEWSPAPERMAN

The first myth was that "States' rights" was the primary dispute that caused the Civil War. True, except for the overriding fact that the right that the Southern states were fighting for was the right to own slaves. Slavery was what the war was about, even for those southerners who didn't own slaves. Perhaps they didn't like the answer to the question "If the Negroes don't pick the cotton, who will?"

Since then "states' rights" has been every state's response to a federal law which they did not like. Many had to be dragged into the 20th century and states' rights was what they dragged their feet with.

Famously, in the years between the Civil War and WWI the Supreme Court often cited states' rights as the argument for overturning much of the progressive legislation of the era.

But now states' rights has taken on new meaning. Large corporations are taking advantage of the fact that there are 50 states, varied in size, power and prosperity. The "full faith and credit" clause of the Constitution basically says that if it's good in one state, it's good in all.

For instance, a marriage license issued in one state is respected by every other state. This was a problem when gay marriage was first allowed in some states but not others. Some states refused to recognize a gay marriage from another state. The Supreme Court eventually cleaned this up, making gay marriage legal in all 50 states.

That's all a distraction from the real issue. The real issue is that large banks and other corporations are incorporating in tiny states like Delaware and South Dakota and using advantageous laws, often of their own crafting, to further their business interests. These states vigorously encourage these companies to incorporate in their states to attract fees for the state coffers.

Imagine how little lobbying money it takes to influence the legislature in Delaware as opposed to New York or California. Imagine Exxon being sued by the State of Delaware. Who has the larger team of lawyers and resources to pursue a large lawsuit? This comes in handy when you want to defend a major oil spill case.

Banks incorporated in a state like South Dakota may issue a credit card with terms and interest rates that would never be acceptable in Massachusetts or Ohio but must be honored under the "full faith and credit" clause of the Constitution.

The latest and greatest states' rights manipulation comes from the National Rifle Association (NRA) which hopes to pass a concealed carry law through the Congress which says that one state's concealed carry permit must be honored by all fifty states, in effect letting Alabama tell New York who can carry a concealed weapon on New Year's Eve in Times Square. While it's not getting much traction in the Congress now, a weapons manufacturer can still dream.

This somehow seems to be a perversion of states' rights. I guess this is what they mean by things coming "full circle."

LIE #21

The Supreme Court is the final "Law of the Land."

"My biggest problem with modernity may lie in the growing separation of the ethical and the legal"
NASSIM NICHOLAS TALEB (1960-PRESENT), THE BED OF PROCRUSTES: PHILOSOPHICAL AND PRACTICAL APHORISMS

We were all taught in school that the U.S. Supreme Court was the court of final resolution. Lower court cases eventually, through the appeals process, worked their way to the Supreme Court where a final ruling would be made. It was final in the sense that there would be no more appeals. It would thereafter be the "law of the land." We were all taught this, but is it true?

Let's look at that statement again through two landmark cases of the second half of the 20th century; 1954 Brown vs Board of Education and 1973 Roe vs Wade.

The 1954 Brown vs Board of Education decision ended segregation in public schools once and for all. Many schools in the North and most in the South either refused to implement the ruling or dragged their feet. In Little Rock, Arkansas, President Eisenhower called out the National Guard to insure the safety of the black students brave enough to integrate the central high school. Prince Georges County in Virginia eventually closed their public schools rather than integrate. Most white students went to private academies while black students were forced to stay with out-of-county relatives. No harm done? Fifty years later, the number one occupation in this county is food preparer, as in McDonald's and Burger King or chicken plucking. School desegregation dragged on for twenty years, well into the 1970s with conflicts throughout the South and North.

The 1973 Roe vs Wade decision guaranteed a woman's right to an abortion in all fifty states. Until that ruling, abortion was only legal in a handful of states.

After 1973, states opposed to abortion went about the business of compromising a woman's right to an abortion through a never-ending series of legislative initiatives. Clinic sizes, hallway sizes, doctor's admitting privileges at local hospitals have all been legislated to disrupt the provision of this service. Abortion clinics have had to navigate a legal minefield just to stay open, while clinic employees have risked their lives to provide this service. Doctors have been killed, clinics have been bombed and employees have been constantly threatened with violence.

Some of the net results of all this activity is that Mississippi now has one clinic performing the procedure and the vast state of Texas is down to less than a handful. Many other states have followed suit. Women are forced to endure expensive travel, unnecessary waiting periods, and invasive testing designed to discourage a woman from having an abortion.

All this has been done without a word from the Supreme Court. If the net result of all this harassment and litigation is to make abortions practically non-existent, despite the Court's 1973 decision, I guess the Court is fine with that!

Now, instead of accepting the ruling of the court, those opposed to a ruling lobby for judges sympathetic to their position to be appointed to the court. These days there is always another test case and it only takes one favorable decision to reverse decades of precedent.

The United States, which in our lifetime has always been the world's most litigious society is determined to separate us from the runner-up nation by an even larger margin. Once again, we're #1.

"And ultimate truth, if, indeed, it exists, is rarely recognizable in the endless rows of long words that crowd page after page of most judicial regurgitations."
GERRY SPENCE, HOW TO ARGUE & WIN EVERY TIME: AT HOME, AT WORK, IN COURT, EVERYWHERE, EVERYDAY

LIE #22
Pro-choice, Pro-life Abortion Positions have equal support

"I want any young men who buy a gun to be treated like young women who seek an abortion. Think about it: a mandatory 48 hour waiting period, written permission from a parent or judge, a note from a doctor proving he knows what he is about to do, time spent watching a video on individual and mass murders, traveling hundreds of miles at his own expense to get to the nearest gun shop, and walking through protesters holding photos of loved ones killed by guns and being called a murderer."
GLORIA STEINEM (1934-PRESENT) - WOMAN

I'd like to dispel a few myths on abortion. People deceive themselves on this issue all the time. Let me start with this: No one uses abortion for birth control. Women use birth control methods for birth control. No one who carries a baby into the 7th, 8th or 9th month of a pregnancy wants an abortion. They just don't. Ninety-five percent of people want there to be few or no abortions, therefore, Pro-life. Most, but surprisingly not all of those, believe that women should have access to high-quality sex education and birth control.

Unwanted pregnancies occur for three reasons: 1) disregard for birth control. In the passion of the moment, birth control was never a consideration, or not available, or poor sex education regarding likelihood of pregnancy 2) birth control failed. The rhythm method may have been miscalculated, condom failed or birth control pill forgotten. 3) unwanted sexual contact, as in rape or incest.

In all these instances no one, or almost no one, wants the government to make the choice on whether they should have an abortion. Therefore, 95%, or more, are against the government deciding whether "we" should have an abortion, that is, Pro-Choice.

The disagreement comes in when we discuss the abortions of "Others." *"Others"* have unwanted pregnancies because they are careless or immoral. "We" got pregnant due to bad luck or circumstances beyond our control. Others' reasons for abortion are an unwillingness to face the consequences of their actions, or a disregard for human life.

Our reason for an abortion is "it's the only viable option, considering our special circumstances."

Almost all of us have a threshold where an abortion is acceptable. The highest is perhaps to save the life of the mother. An abortion after rape or incest may be acceptable, or perhaps to save a family when one partner is unfaithful. Maybe it's when your daughter is pregnant at 16 and college sports scholarships are out the window; or worse, when your daughter is 14 or 13. Most of us have a rationale where abortion is an option. None of us want the state to make that decision for us. None of us are sure how we would react in these situations. I can't believe you think otherwise.

"The state must declare the child to be the most precious treasure of the people. As long as the government is perceived as working for the benefit of the children, the people will happily endure almost any curtailment of liberty and almost any deprivation."
ADOLF HITLER(1889-1945)-TIME MAGAZINE'S MAN OF THE CENTURY, 20TH CENTURY

LIE #23

We can replace fossil fuels with other forms of energy

"Problems cannot be solved at the same level of awareness that created them."
ALBERT EINSTEIN (1879-1955) A VERY STABLE GENIUS

What is the human energy equivalence to a barrel of oil? Surprisingly, it's not an easy answer in that the energy in the oil can do things no amount of humans can do, like propel a car down a road at 60 MPH or light a city, and the oil doesn't need to sleep, eat or rest.

Rather than debating the correct number, let's give it a range of 3,000 to 23,000 man-hours. While the range is large, 3,000 man-hours is a year and a half of work, and by work I don't mean sitting at a computer designing websites. I mean 3,000 hours of chopping down trees or carrying water or some other exhausting task.

Incredible, isn't it? That's why any talk of giving up oil, whether it's about global warming or exhausting the supply, quickly becomes a discussion nobody really wants to have. And if nobody wants to have it, politicians certainly don't want to discuss it. We just keep kicking it down the road. Of course, that's not what we call it, but that's what it is. We say that new technology will bring new supplies. Although that is true, what does this new oil cost? The easy oil has already been found and new discoveries involve deeper and deeper offshore drilling, or fracking oil shale, or removing the oil from the Canadian tar sands. This is all costly and potentially catastrophic to the ecosystem.

Climate change is controversial for all those people attached in one way or another to the status quo of oil. For the rest of us, it's just common sense. Pumping millions of tons of carbon dioxide and methane into the atmosphere every year has to have an effect. Scientists tell us that the effect is to heat the oceans and the atmosphere, and that is changing the climate. Certainly there are other factors to consider. Solar activity goes in cycles making things hotter or colder. Volcanic eruptions spewing ash into the atmosphere can have a cooling effect, as happened with Mt. Tambora in 1815, causing 1816 to be the year without a summer.

Nature doesn't work in a straight line or smooth curve but most of the hottest years on record have occurred recently and the carbon dioxide numbers keep going up. That is fact!

No one wants to do the work that all our oil and electric-based devices now do. Only a few hundred years ago that's how all work was done. We are way too soft and spoiled for that. Still, the question remains: "What will we do when oil is no longer the answer and how long do we have to decide?"

Environmentalist Bill McKibben and others started a website in 2008 called "350.org." The 350 stood for 350 parts per million (ppm) of carbon dioxide in the atmosphere. That number represented an amount that would stop global temperature rise. We are now at 400 ppm and talking about limiting temperature rise only two degrees Celsius, yet no agreements have been reached to slow this down.

Scientists estimate we can put **565** gigatons (one gigaton equals a billion tons) of carbon into the atmosphere and keep global temperature rise to two degrees. Fossil fuel companies currently have **2,795** gigatons of carbon reserves, and they don't get paid to keep it in the ground. See? See how hard this all is?

> "Whether we and our politicians know it or not, Nature is party to all our deals and decisions, and she has more votes, a longer memory, and a sterner sense of justice than we do."
> ENVIRONMENTALIST WENDELL BERRY (1934-PRESENT)

LIE #24

American Exceptionalism?

"...the more I see, the better satisfied I am that I am an American; free born and free bred, where I acknowledge no man as my superior, except for his own worth, or as my inferior, except for his own demerit."
THEODORE ROOSEVELT (1858-1919), 26TH PRESIDENT PHILOSOPHICAL AND PRACTICAL APHORISMS

American exceptionalism? American ignorance? American arrogance? I don't know what to call it. Are Americans so much smarter than the rest of world that all discussion of problems and potential solutions must never mention the rest of the world? I am not saying that our problems are exactly the same as the rest of the world nor are their solutions superior to ours, but where relevant, shouldn't the views and solutions of the rest of the world occasionally enter the conversation?

America is currently debating whether and how much to raise the minimum wage. What is it in France? Germany? Scandinavia? What effect does it have?

America is currently debating income inequality. Is that debate happening in the rest of the world? Is income inequality worsening in Europe or declining? What are they doing about it?

America has over 1 ½ million people incarcerated. How does that compare to Europe? Are our sentences longer or shorter? Do our prisoners return to prison more often or less so?

Climate change is an international issue. Do their scientists agree with ours? Do their governments agree with the scientific consensus and are they doing something about it? What?

Healthcare in the U.S. has been an important political topic for years now. How do the different countries of Europe deal with it? Do they all have universal health care? How do they pay for it?

Don't you think the Germans or the British or the Japanese might have a helpful hint on these and other subjects or are they just stupid? The great thing about two big oceans between us and the rest of the world is that they make it easy to close our eyes and pretend that the rest of the world doesn't exist. Easy, but not very smart.

"Our myths are so many, our vision so dim, our self-deception so deep and our smugness so gross that scarcely any way now remains of reporting the American Century except from behind the billboards ..."
NELSON ALGREN (1909-1981) AUTHOR

The Fourth Pillar of Democracy:
Immigration

"All the problems we face in the United States today can be traced to an unenlightened immigration policy on the part of the American Indian."
PAT PAULSEN (1927-1997) - HUMORIST

The U.S. is better than any country in the world at assimilating immigrants.

We describe ourselves as a nation of immigrants because describing ourselves as a nation of invaders doesn't sound as nice.

Putting aside that the Native Americans were overwhelmed by immigrants and that neither assimilated into the others' culture, those Europeans who came after the initial wave of pilgrims and explorers eventually integrated themselves into the American culture. No matter what language they spoke when they arrived, English became the dominant language either in the first or second generation, and while cultural differences were celebrated at various times of the year, we all claimed to be Americans. It was only much later that terms like Italian-American, Mexican-American, or African-American came to be used.

The United States does not put the same emphasis on bloodlines for citizenship as do other industrialized societies. American citizenship is much more about ideas and values than ancestry. Anyone in the U.S. can go through the process to become an American citizen.

The U.S., like most of the Western Hemisphere, but unlike most of the rest of the world has birthright citizenship, which entitles anyone born here to automatically be a citizen and have all the rights that citizenship implies.

While people emigrate to the U.S. from all over the world, the majority of our immigrants are now from Mexico and Central America, a large number of which have entered and remain illegally, often with children born in the U.S. and therefore full citizens. This is a problem we have been unable to deal with for many years now.

A path to citizenship for illegal immigrants is described as "Amnesty" by those who wish to send them home. To others, sending an estimated eleven million undocumented immigrants, many of whom have been living here for decades, back to their home countries makes no practical sense.

The United States, like most industrialized countries in the world, need immigration to support aging populations. Low birth rates throughout Western societies and Japan are creating labor shortages and stagnant or negative growth rates. Barring a baby boom, countries with low immigration rates are going to fall behind the rest of the world.

In This Perfect Day, novelist Ira Levin describes a futuristic society where individuals are controlled by a dominant state through drugs and propaganda. A few individuals rebel and, in an attempt to free society, reach the control center, where they are - surprisingly - welcomed with open arms by the current leadership, who have monitored them from the beginning and who expect them to become the future leaders.

This is the tale of immigration. Individuals, deciding to leave their homes to secure a better life, make the difficult journey to a new land. Sometimes they are illegal, sometimes not, but aren't they the people we most want in this country. These are the bold and dynamic souls a vibrant democracy needs.

Fortunately, the United States is still a very desirable destination. The "Shining City on the Hill" still attracts the best and the brightest from around the world.

> *"The land flourished because it was fed from so many sources--because it was nourished by so many cultures and traditions and peoples."*
> PRESIDENT LYNDON B. JOHNSON AT THE STATUE OF LIBERTY, 10/03/1965

SECTION V
The Social Fabric of America

"The simple fact of the matter is that the world has never built a multi-ethnic democracy in which no particular ethnic group is in the majority and where political equality, social equality and economic empowerment all have been achieved. This is America's great challenge. We cannot retreat from it."
DANIELLE ALLEN (1971-PRESENT) ETHICIST

LIE #25

We live in a Post Racial Society

"They made us many promises, more than I can remember, but they never kept but one; they promised to take our land, and they took it"
LAKOTA CHIEF RED CLOUD (1822-1909)

What is the lie about race? It is all a lie. We have lied about race since 1492 and we have continued to lie about it in one form or another for more than 500 years.

When the first Europeans arrived in the New World they did not see Native Americans as a different but equal cultural group. They saw them as a group to be exploited or a rival to be eliminated.

Hundreds of years of near constant warfare among themselves gave the Europeans an advantage in weaponry, not the most obvious example of being more "civilized" than the natives. This advantage, along with a seemingly endless supply of new settlers, and diseases, doomed the natives.

Unable to enslave the natives, they forced them onto poorer and poorer plots of land and when that land became desirable, as it did when the Osage Tribe struck oil in Oklahoma, the white men made every attempt to cheat them out of it.

Black Africans were imported into the colonies as slaves in 1619. As many as six or seven million more followed to work on the tobacco, rice and indigo plantations along the eastern coast from Maryland to Georgia. Tales of what they called "The Middle Passage" speak of unbelievably horrible and inhumane conditions aboard slave ships, with the destination being thousands of miles and an ocean away from home. The reality of slavery was that land owners could work their slaves especially hard while offering just "the bare necessities of life." Slaves would pick five or six hundred pounds of cotton per day, three times what paid workers would produce. Of course "negative incentives," especially the whip, accounted for much of this extraordinary output.

Lies among the whites began at the very beginning and continued right through the Civil War. Accepted "facts" included "The Negroes really seemed to like cotton picking" and "Fortunately, the Negro is a cheerful being." Whites commonly claimed that neither black men nor women had strong parental feelings toward their offspring. I guess that made it easier to buy and sell and split families.

Many a southern planter was convinced his slaves would not leave the plantation when the opportunity arose, knowing that they were better off than free men. The Civil War proved them all wrong.

"Slavery was a positive good," the foundation of "free and stable political institutions." according to southern Senator John C. Calhoun.

Much of American prosperity was derived from the labor of slaves.

Some Northerners opposed to slavery felt perhaps that some men needed to remain enslaved so that others might be free (as long as they, themselves, were among the free.)

Abraham Lincoln, The Great Emancipator, weighed in with "I have no purpose to introduce political and social equality between the white and black races....I am in favor of the race to which I belong having the superior position." – Debate with Stephen Douglas, 1858

Lincoln soon laid out his own resettlement plans. He had selected Chiriqui, a resource-poor area in what is now Panama, to be the new home for millions of African Americans. Lincoln just had to convince them to leave. In August of 1862 he lectured five black leaders that it was their duty, given what their people had done to the United States, to accept the exodus to South America, telling them "But for your race among us there could not be war."

Race Part 2:

Promised forty acres and a mule (they never got the mule, or the forty acres), emancipated slaves began to build a life and a community under the protective umbrella of the Union army. "Reconstruction" featured a strong desire for education and a place in the American political system. During Reconstruction blacks voted at an all-time high, electing local, state and federal officials.

The white population, self-deluded as to the inferiority of their former slaves, bided their time until the northern states became tired of supporting the army in the south. The contested presidential election of Rutherford Hayes in 1876 led to the "Compromise of 1877," in which the south agreed to Hayes as President in exchange for self-rule and the end of the Union Army in the south. Goodbye Reconstruction – Hello Jim Crow.

Laws suppressing black votes and black rights continued for the next 90 years, lynchings for almost as long. The south, under the banner of "states' rights," foiled all attempts by the federal government to provide a measure of civil rights for blacks.

The northern states and the federal government were not blameless here. As blacks moved from the hopelessness of the south, they were forced into segregated housing, excluded from good paying union jobs and generally treated as second class citizens.

Social Security, passed into law in 1935, excluded agricultural workers and domestic workers, the two largest employment categories for minorities.

The G.I. Bill of 1944, generally regarded as the most important legislation to come out of the 1940s, provided educational opportunities and low-cost mortgages to returning veterans, thus setting the stage for the economic boom of the 1950s. The G.I. Bill was crafted to accommodate the Jim Crow laws of the south, and as such was administered by local officials who excluded most blacks from educational grants and low-cost mortgages.

The Civil Rights Act of 1964, along with the Voting Rights Act have improved black lives, but blacks still trail significantly in the statistics on employment, earnings, and wealth.

"Blacks are always talking about the south, the south. If you are below the Canadian border, you are in the South." – Malcolm X

While Europeans arrived in America, forcing the Indians west, and imported black slaves from Africa, labor was still needed on the west coast. Chinese laborers were imported to help build the Transcontinental Railroad. With an economic downturn after the Civil War, Chinese "coolies" were blamed for depressed wages, which brought the "Chinese Exclusion Act of 1882", the first time an entire ethnic group was banned from the U.S. Made permanent in 1902, it endured until 1943, when the Magnusen Act granted 105 (wow!) Chinese visas a year.

Japanese immigrants arrived on the west coast until the Asian Exclusion Act of 1924 and were generally successful, becoming farmers and small businessmen. This did not prevent west coast Japanese from being rounded up and transferred to the nation's interior during war with Japan. Never mind that these were American citizens. Never mind that German and Italian Americans never left their homes along the Atlantic coast. The Japanese, non-white, presented a clear and present danger. White supremacy - the unchallenged, unspoken rule of America for hundreds of years - is only now being discussed. Whites, for the first time in our history may soon lose their majority status, and that certainly makes many of them nervous. Why? Here's a clue.

Plantation owners in the antebellum south were constantly worried about slave revolts. Their unspoken fear was that the freed slaves would treat their former masters as their masters had treated them. This terrified them, as it should have. In the words of Thomas Jefferson: "I tremble for my country when I reflect that God is just: that his justice cannot sleep forever."

LIE #26

We want a country of equal opportunity, not equal outcomes.

"Most men are a little better than their circumstances give them a chance to be."
WILLIAM FAULKNER (1897-1962) SOUTHERN WRITER

I don't know about you, but I *never* hear anyone proposing equal outcomes for all, so this statement is just ridiculous. It has the advantage of making "equal opportunity for all" sound far more reasonable. The truth is, however, that the whole statement is false. We don't want equal outcomes, but we also don't want equal opportunity for all, no matter what we say. We would like an advantage, an edge, a headstart and we will go to great efforts to get it.

Whether it's in our careers, with our kids, or even in our games, we want to win. The easiest, surest way to win is to have an edge. In business we try to get the tax break, the inside track on a bid, or inside knowledge on the competition. If possible, we send our kids to the best schools, the best coaches, and get them extra help if needed, with little or no thought for the other kids.

In New York City, eight specialized high schools, including Brooklyn Tech and Bronx Science, have one standard admissions test. Highly competitive, these schools have a disproportionately low number of Black and Hispanic children. A proposal to admit students based on grades and class and citywide standing was vigorously opposed by those who successfully navigate the current test. Never mind that this test is no better indicator of future success than any other.

America's favorite sports team is the New York Yankees, a team famous for its many championships, achieved in no small measure by buying up the very best talent at prices no one else could afford. This fact does not matter to a Yankee fan; in fact, they are rather proud of it.

Life is not fair, and equal opportunity is rarely equal, no matter how laudable a goal it is. In "The Sports Gene," author David Epstein highlights individuals with genetic advantages for certain sports that have propelled them to Olympic success. Examples include abnormally high levels of testosterone in female athletes or increased red blood cells for competitors in endurance events. In every instance, the athlete downplayed the genetic advantage, pointing out the many, many hours of training and hard work they had put in. I have no doubt that in every instance it was true. No one wins Olympic Gold without dedication and hard work. I also have no doubt that they were not the only ones dedicated and willing to work hard.

In our personal narrative, we often downplay our advantages or our good fortune in favor of a tale of overcoming obstacles. Sometimes we aren't even aware of our advantages; everyone's story is different.

Bill Gates was born in the right year, in the right place with a father who was an engineer for Hewlett-Packard just as computers were jumping into the American consciousness. Was he smart and ambitious and bold? Of course. Was he in the right place at the right time? Of course. Is he aware of that? I hope so.

> *"I know, up on top you are seeing great sights, but down here at the bottom we, too, should have rights."*
> DR. SEUSS (1904 -1991) - YERTLE THE TURTLE AND GERTRUDE MCFUZZ

LIE #27

Americans do not want "Socialized Medicine" like Canada

"Universal coverage, not medical technology, is the foundation of any caring health care system."
RICHARD LAMM (1935-PRESENT), FORMER GOVERNOR, COLORADO

This has to be a lie because most Americans know almost nothing about Canadian healthcare, and what they think they know has been provided by vested interests in the U.S.; and may not even be true.

I'll try to stick to the numbers and avoid the subjective analysis. I believe these are accurate as of 2013.

The U.S. spent 17.1% of GDP on healthcare, compared to 10.7% for Canada. That's more than 50% more for the U.S. and unlike Canada, not everyone is covered. In 1980, most developed countries were within a percentage point or two of each other. That's when the U.S. took off and is now at 17.1% with France, the next highest, at 11.6%.

Canadians and Americans have approximately the same number of doctors per capita. Americans see their doctors 4.0 times a year while Canadians see a doctor 7.7 times a year.

Americans get twice as many high-tech scans as Canadians, and many more MRI or CT scans than any other country except Japan.

Americans (2.2) and Canadians (1.8) are at the high end for number of prescriptions routinely taken, but those prescriptions cost 50% less in Canada.

The U.S. (6.1) and Canada (4.8) were first and third in infant mortality (bad), and first and second in seniors with two or more chronic conditions(also bad.)

Canadians come out better in all categories except high-tech scans and waiting time for elective surgery while spending 50% less and covering everyone. There are 44,000 deaths each year in the U.S. attributed to inadequate or unaffordable treatment and medical bills are the number one reason for personal bankruptcy.

The American Medical Association (AMA), the drug companies and others have convinced the U.S. population that they will lose their doctor and have long waiting lines for treatment if we adopt a system similar to Canada's.

With almost twice as many doctor's visits annually in Canada, long waiting lines for treatment may not be a concern, nor should losing your doctor. It is true that there are likely longer waits for elective surgery in Canada. No co-pays, no incomprehensible bills, and universal coverage. All for 50% less than we pay now. What's not to like?

American healthcare recipients fall into several categories. The first group is those who have employer provided healthcare. Their satisfaction is based on the size of employer contributions and cost of deductibles, and their concern about job security, for insurance goes away if the job goes away.

The second group receives government paid healthcare through Medicare, the Veteran's Administration and Medicaid for the poor.

The third group consists of those who have to find healthcare on the open market. This is the group Obamacare helps the most with subsidies and guaranteed coverage for pre-existing conditions.

There is one more group, the uninsured, who are uninsured for a variety of reasons such as cost, pre-existing conditions, or a lack of imagination regarding misfortune.

Your opposition to changes to the current healthcare system is directly related to which group you are in. Healthcare paid by your employer while you have job security makes you likely to be unwilling to change. You don't want to wait for that knee replacement.

All the other groups would like to see some degree of change except Medicare recipients, who already are part of socialized medicine.

Greater job insecurity, ever higher premiums, greater deductibles and co-pays all make socialized medicine a more appealing option for more people than our current system. Of course Americans hate the word "socialized."

Many Americans like the healthcare they have. Many are afraid of the cost of a change to the system. Remember, we already pay 50% more than anyone else with mediocre results and nowhere near universal coverage. Many other countries besides Canada have achieved universal coverage at an affordable cost. Why is the U.S. the only one who cannot?

America's health care system is neither healthy, caring, nor a system.
WALTER CRONKITE (1916-2009) - LEGENDARY TV ANCHORMAN

LIE #28

America is the Moral Leader of the world

"Our moral authority is as important, if not more important, than our troop strength or our high-tech weapons. We are rapidly losing that moral authority, not only in the Arab world but all over the world."
ROBERT REICH (1946-PRESENT) FORMER LABOR SECRETARY (1993-1997)

As the world's oldest continuous democracy and the home of The Statue of Liberty, the United States has often been viewed as Ronald Reagan's "Shining City on a Hill," a beacon for all the world, a noble place for all the world's hopes and aspirations. No more.

As a moral leader you would think that the U.S. would be in the forefront of most international efforts to make the world a better place. That turns out to not be the case.

When it comes to international treaties the U.S. has signed very few and ratified even fewer, many of which have the support of an overwhelming majority of nations.

Among those unsigned or unratified - stop me if one sounds morally objectionable - we begin with the International Labor Organization's 1930 Forced Labor Convention and the 1948-49 conventions on collective bargaining and the right to organize: one would stop slavery and indentured servitude, the other would allow workers to obtain some bargaining rights through organization. In 1951 there was the Convention on the Status of Refugees; we signed the amended version in 1967, but did not ratify. In 1972 there was the Anti-Ballistic Missile Treaty which was intended to prevent defensive weapons nullifying the Mutually Assured Destruction (MAD) nature of nuclear weapons. We ratified it, but withdrew in 2002, citing new defensive technologies that we would be willing to pass on to the Russians. That hasn't gone well as the Russians saw it as an aggressive act (we didn't give them the technology either.)

1991 saw the United Nations Law of the Sea Convention, which the U.S. did not sign, along with less than 20 other countries, compared to the 167 that did. In 1997 we chose not to join in the Anti-Personnel Mine Convention, which made our denial of the 2008 Cluster Munition Convention at least seem consistent. We couldn't see our way to abandoning those munitions that killed and maimed thousands - often children - long after the conflict was over. 1998 brought us The Rights of the Child Convention which we signed but did not ratify, the only country on the planet not to do so. Ratification would have meant subjecting the U.S. to international law in matters involving the treaty, something which the U.S. currently will not do. So, of course, we did not ratify 1998's International Criminal Court either.

Finally, we have withdrawn from the Paris Agreement on Climate Change.

I do not doubt that many of these agreements, and the many other agreements not mentioned and also not ratified, were flawed documents with one or more disagreeable statements that many countries found not to their liking. Unlike the United States, most of those other countries wound up signing and ratifying the treaties despite their flaws. I understand how hard it must be to get an international agreement ratified in this partisan Congress, but Canada and most of the European Union signed most of these treaties and Conventions that the U.S. decided to reject. The Paris Climate Accord managed to get the agreement of every country on the planet except the U.S. and war-torn Syria. Then Syria signed on, leaving only the U.S., with its entirely indefensible position of climate change denial. I asked you to stop reading if any of these treaties sounded objectionable. I see that you are still with me.

How can we be a moral leader when we refuse to be a part of the international movement to improve the world by banning munitions and land mines that kill kids, or promote the human rights of women and children, or help to stop global catastrophe due to climate change? I don't think we are that moral leader, and without significant change, I don't think we can be.

> *"The essence of immorality is to make an exception of myself."*
> JANE ADDAMS (1860-1935) - SOCIAL REFORMER

LIE #29

We are all in this together

"It is our choices that show what we truly are, far more than our abilities."
J.K. ROWLING (1965-PRESENT)-AUTHOR, HARRY POTTER SERIES

One of the great myths of this country is that we are all Americans, and as such, we are all in this together, whatever "this" is.

September 11, 2001, was the day we all truly came together. Not only were we all together, but on that day much of the rest of the world declared they were Americans as well. That sentiment lasted until March 20, 2003, when we first bombed Baghdad, signaling the beginning of the Iraq war, a war many felt was necessary and many did not.

Millions marched in the streets around the world in protest, in hope of preventing a war, but failed on that March evening. The world went from "We are all Americans now!" to being for or against the war.

On that evening America divided as well, and we have remained divided on that issue, and many others, ever since.

Besides being divided on the Iraq war, we are divided into the haves and have-nots, rural and urban, white and non-white, multicultural and nativist, and so many others I can't keep track.

What I find distressing about this division is not that we are divided -I'm a person of strong opinions who doesn't mind being challenged- but that programs and policies that might be good for the country are still opposed if they help those in the other camp; Democrats and Republicans are opposed to good policies if the other party is seen as receiving credit.

Natives, being opposed to immigrants, cite an unwillingness to pay the costs associated with assimilation, such as job training and language skills. Never mind that they, or their families at some time were in the same boat as these immigrants and managed to become self-sufficient taxpayers within a generation or less.

City dwellers are unwilling to help pay the greater costs of rural infrastructure. FDR's Rural Electrification Program might not be possible today. Rural citizens are unwilling to pay for mass transit in the cities. White welfare recipients outnumber black, but whites are unwilling to support programs that benefit non-working (I meant "lazy") blacks. If one unqualified person benefits from a program, that's reason enough to cancel it. Never mind if the principal beneficiaries are children. Anecdotal evidence abounds of food stamp recipients loading up their shopping carts with steak and lobster while the hard-working family has hamburger. I didn't know blacks were so fond of lobster. Despite blacks' stereotypical affinity for fried chicken, I have never heard a story of a shopping cart filled with chicken paid with food stamps.

Everyone wants to send their kids to college, yet so many complain of political correctness on campus, much of which occurs at America's elite universities - the very schools parents are begging to accept their children.

Two congressmen under indictment, one for misuse of campaign funds and one for insider trading, and a senator tried for corruption ending in a mistrial and censured by the ethics committee, were re-elected, presumably to keep the seats from falling into the other party's hands. Republicans believe Barack Obama was not born in the U.S. Democrats think George W. Bush had something to do with 9/11. In 2016 too many people, including one deranged gunman, believed Hillary Clinton was running a child sex ring from a pizzeria in Washington, D.C. Is anything beyond belief if it speaks badly of the other side?

Where does it all end. In every crisis there is an opportunity. I hope it does not take an event as horrific as September 11th, 2001 to bring us together again.

Conclusion

"Not everything that is faced can be changed, but nothing can be changed until it is faced."
JAMES BALDWIN (1924-1987) - AUTHOR

What do I want you to take from this book? I wish we would all think a little more critically. In this age of news from so many sources, it is important to not accept as fact everything you hear or read. Sources matter, and that which sounds preposterous probably is. Take the time to sort it out. Please do not indiscriminately forward everything you receive online. Act as if "you" are the source and "your" credibility is on the line.

Conspiracy theories abound. Governments will always have secrets and will spin that which they cannot hide, but only facts are facts, and as I said earlier, there are no "alternative facts."

We are a great country, but even great countries have flaws. Pointing them out does not make you less patriotic; denying them does. Be strong in your opposition to lies and half-truths. It's the only way we can have a meaningful discussion about our future. It might be the only way we'll even have a future.

Oh, and one more thing ...

The Fifth Pillar of Democracy:
Charity

"Wherever I find decency and humanity in the world, it reminds me of America"
KURT WEIL – 1947, GERMAN PLAYWRIGHT

In our current era of turmoil it's very easy to forget that Americans are, and have always been among the most generous people on the planet. In 1812 the very young United States sent relief aid for a famine in Venezuela.

The United States sent frigates full of relief supplies to Ireland during the famine of 1846-47. This was all private aid as the constitutionality of sending government aid was still undecided. Some contributions were made in the hope that this would reduce Irish immigration to the U.S., but the Irish did not care why the Americans were being so generous. (This may be an idea for our current Central American immigration situation.)

Throughout our history we have sent aid in whatever form necessary to disasters throughout the world. The American military is always among the first responders at natural disasters, bringing unique skills to bear on whatever the flood, earthquake, hurricane or other disaster demands. That is often followed by food, clothing, medical supplies and cash donations to aid the victims.

The Marshall Plan was our largest and most successful charitable contribution ever. The U.S. sent over $13 Billion to 17 countries in Europe to help rebuild after the Second World War. That sum represented 5% of U.S. domestic product. That would be about $400 Billion in today's dollars. As difficult as life was in Europe after WWII, the Marshall Plan helped save the continent from further destruction, chaos and war.

There was relief aid to Indonesia after the tsunami in 2004, the aid to Haiti after the earthquake in 2010. These disasters killed 200,000 and 300,000 people, respectively, and wiped out entire towns. The U.S. raised millions in relief aid from ordinary citizens.

A different example is President George W. Bush's President's Emergency Plan for AIDS Relief (PEPFAR). Congress approved $15 Billion over five years for AIDS treatment and assistance for twelve sub-Saharan African countries and support for the millions of children orphaned by the disease. It was considered the world's largest-ever initiative to combat one disease. The program was increased to $39 Billion in 2007 for the next five years and continued throughout the Obama presidency, saving over one million lives and improving the mortality rate in those countries by as much as 20%.

U.S. citizens are equally generous at home, contributing more to local churches than any other country and finishing first or second in the World Giving Index (second to Myanmar?) every year in this decade. Americans donated $410 Billion to charity in 2017.

In some countries the government takes over the responsibility for many public needs, something that the U.S. does privately. A conservative argument against greater government participation in charity is that it is unnecessary, considering the large amount contributed privately. But is it unnecessary? Ask any food bank if they have enough food.

Despite many of the conflicts the United States has throughout the world, American charity is a constant that keeps the world looking favorably on us.

"We never think lightly of those who walk with us on our uphill days."
RICHELLE E. GOODRICH, AUTHOR SMILE ANYWAY

Recommended Reading List

I promised you 8,000 pages and hundreds of notes. Here they are.

Makers and Takers: The Rise of Finance and the Fall of American Business - Rana Faroohar

The Fifth Risk by Michael Lewis 2018

The Healing of America: A Global Quest for Better, Cheaper, and Fairer Health Care by T. R. Reid, August 2010

A Fine Mess: A Global Quest for a Simpler, Fairer, and More Efficient Tax System by T. R. Reid, April, 2018

America's Bitter Pill: Money, Politics, Backroom Deals, and the Fight to Fix Our Broken Healthcare System by Steven Brill, August 2015

Tailspin: The People and Forces Behind America's Fifty-Year Fall--and Those Fighting to Reverse It by Steven Brill, May 2018

The Uninhabitable Earth: Life After Warming by David Wallace-Wells, February 2019

Poor Economics: A Radical Rethinking of the Way to Fight Global Poverty by Abhijit Banerjee and Esther Duflo, March 2012

Why Nations Fail: The Origins of Power, Prosperity, and Poverty by Daron Acemoglu and James Robinson, December 2013

Plutocrats: The Rise of the New Global Super-Rich and the Fall of Everyone Else by Chrystia Freeland, September 2013

The Fall of the House of Dixie: The Civil War and the Social Revolution That Transformed the South by Bruce Levine 2012

White Rage: The Unspoken Truth of Our Racial Divide by Carol Anderson, September 2017

The Sports Gene: Inside the Science of Extraordinary Athletic Performance by David Epstein, April 2014

Capital in the Twenty-first Century by Thomas Piketty and Arthur Goldhammer, August 2017

Scarcity: The New Science of Having Less and How It Defines Our Lives by Sendhil Mullainathanand Eldar Shafir, November 2014

Nudge: Improving Decisions about Health, Wealth, and Happiness by Richard Thaler and Cass Sunstein 2009

Flash Boys: A Wall Street Revolt by Michael Lewis 2015

Made in the USA
Middletown, DE
20 November 2019